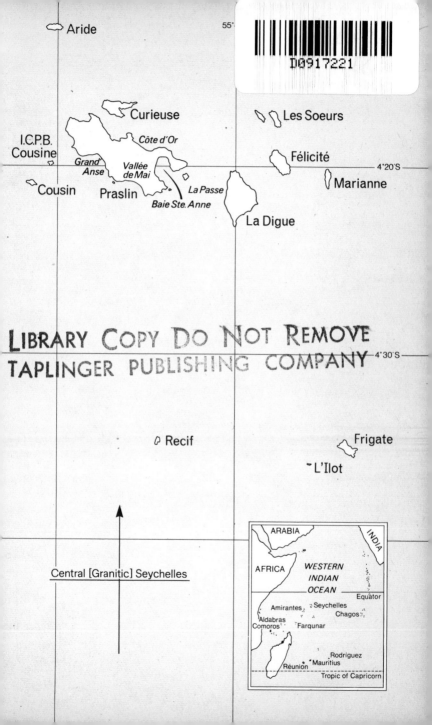

Aride

55°

D0917221

Curieuse

Les Soeurs

Côte d'Or

I.C.P.B.
Cousine

Félicité

4°20'S

Grand
Anse

Vallée
de Mai

Marianne

Cousin

Praslin

La Passe

Baie Ste. Anne

La Digue

4°30'S

Recif

Frigate

L'Ilot

Central [Granitic] Seychelles

ARABIA

INDIA

AFRICA

WESTERN
INDIAN
OCEAN

Equator

Amirantes

Seychelles

Chagos

Aldabras
Comoros

Farqunar

Rodriguez

Réunion

Mauritius

Tropic of Capricorn

The Birds of Seychelles
and the Outlying Islands

The Birds of Seychelles

and the Outlying Islands

Malcolm Penny

with 12 plates
and line drawings by
CHLOË TALBOT-KELLY

A Taplinger Worldwide Field Guide
TAPLINGER PUBLISHING CO., INC.
NEW YORK

First published in the United States in 1974 by
TAPLINGER PUBLISHING CO., INC.
New York, New York

Library of Congress Catalog Card Number: 74-5811
ISBN 0-8008-2712-0

Contents

Plates

Preface

Seychelles remains one of the least disturbed island groups, and one of the last to be studied by ornithologists. At the same time as interest in conservation is growing among the islands, a new wave of expansion is flooding over the Colony as the airport permits the growth of the tourist industry.

This book is intended to serve two purposes at once: as a repository of the accumulated knowledge about the birds of Seychelles it should act as an introduction for the professional naturalist working in the islands; and as a description of the fascinating birds to be seen among the Paradise Islands it might entice and later instruct the traveller. I met many of the visitors who were at the front of the tourist wave in the cruise ship *Lindblad Explorer*, and it is with them and their questions in mind that I have written the text.

Quite apart from merely being able to put a name to a bird – itself a curiously satisfying achievement – people want to know how the creature lives, what it feeds on in such small islands, when it breeds in a place which has virtually no seasons, and how many there are of the great rarities. I have tried to answer these questions, and such others as have arisen during conversations with interested birders and others in the islands.

To too many of these questions the honest answer is 'I don't know': but someone will find out one day – and that is what the margins and flyleaves are for in a book of this kind.

Acknowledgements

I wrote the first draft of this book on Cousin Island while I was working for the International Council for Bird Preservation. It was done principally for my own satisfaction, but partly at the prompting of Roger Tory Peterson, Guy Mountfort, and others on the *Lindblad Explorer* who had noticed the need for it. I hope that they recognise their godchild.

I am indebted to the organisations which have taken me repeatedly to the Indian Ocean to work on the birds: the University of Bristol Expeditions Society, the Royal Society Expedition to Aldabra, and ICBP, as well as Lindblad Travel Inc. of New York, who actually paid me to tell other people about the islands I love. My teacher and guide, in the museum as well as in the field, has been Con Benson, whose patience and kindness is responsible for any accuracy and clarity in these pages; Bill Bourne encouraged me during the worst stage, the rewriting of the first draft; and he and Tony Diamond gave invaluable advice during the writing of the seabird section. Tony Diamond was a very welcome companion on Aldabra during the expedition (even if he did persuade me to collect Booby vomitus while he held the chicks). Guy Lionnet, Philippe Lalanne, and others of the Department of Agriculture in Seychelles have been continuously helpful, and Tony Beamish and Jack Frazier criticised earlier drafts most pertinently. The contribution of Chloë Talbot Kelly's pictures is obvious, and I cannot thank her enough.

I want also to record my thanks to those Seychellois of my acquaintance, whose ingenuity, generosity, and endless good humour have made their islands my second home. Will Germain, the manager of Cousin since its foundation as a sanctuary, and his wife Christianne stand out; but Harry Charles and Georges Marie, my constant companions on Aldabra, and Will's assistants, Raymond, Alton and Antoine must also be mentioned. To them and to their grandchildren I dedicate this book.

Au peuple Seychellois, mon zamis qui protèze bande zoiseaux lo ziles pli zoli du monde, pour qui mo'ine ecrit ça petit livre. A nous vivre comment frères.

INTRODUCTION

The Islands

'These islands are densely populated with land and sea birds. Among the land birds parrots and finches ravage the crops; Dutch pigeons, doves, and woodpigeons can easily be caught by hand, and make a splendid dish. Also to be seen are blackbirds, orioles, and small magpies; these birds, like the smaller sparrowhawk, are great insect eaters. There is no bird of prey except the large sparrowhawk, which is a menace to poultry. The other birds, such as the sunbirds, white-eyes, flycatchers, and so on, are of interest only to a naturalist.'

Jean Baptiste de Malavois returned from his tour of duty as Military Commandant of Seychelles in 1788, when a naturalist was a rarity, and the majority of people thought of birds either as pests or food, or as uninteresting feathered objects serving only to puzzle us as to the Creator's intentions. De Malavois found a bird population virtually unchanged since it was first commented on by John Jourdain nearly two centuries before: but Jourdain was even less interested, recording merely that birds were numerous, and that Turtle Doves were good to eat and easy to catch.

The islands themselves look rather different now from those known by de Malavois. Round the shores, especially near Victoria, the mangrove swamps have been cut out and drained, and the shore has been reclaimed to build a town and waterside houses. Houses can also be seen perched high up on the hillsides, and the rising moon of the American Tracking Station dominates the skyline. But the view of Mahé from a few miles away must be more or less as he knew it: the great bulk of Trois Frères rearing above the lowland woods, its precipices glinting with trickles of water, and a succession of similar peaks and rugged shoulders marching to the south clad in dark forests. The fact that the lowland woods are now mostly coconuts, and the mountain forests mostly secondary regrowth, does not alter the appearance much: we shall see later its effect on the bird life.

Seychelles is a British Crown Colony lying about five degrees south of the equator, in the middle of the Western Indian Ocean 650 miles north-east of Madagascar. The islands of the central group, about twenty-eight in number with a total land area of seventy-five square miles, are granitic outcrops from a submarine plateau about 16,000 square miles in extent. In places the islands reach between 2,500 and 3,000 feet high. At one time, according to geologists, they were exposed over a much greater area, and this might account for their flora and fauna being uncommonly rich for such isolated islands. The origin of the rocks themselves is something of a mystery. The central Seychelles are the only granitic oceanic islands in the world: from the nature of the granite of which they are composed it can be inferred that the islands did not originate in mid-ocean, but were once attached to a continental land-mass. The most likely theory is that they are the crests of a ridge of land left behind when India and Africa swung apart during the drift of the continents. They may have been completely submerged at some time since then. But now the peaks remain above the surface, sculpted by centuries of trade winds into fantastic shapes, supporting plants, some of which are found nowhere else in the world, and a bird fauna of a dozen unique forms. These birds, which concern us here, are the descendants of Asian and African forms which wandered to the islands in the distant past, to evolve into distinct types, some of them so specialised as to defy accurate tracing of their line of descent.

Before we consider the birds themselves, it is worth considering the islands where they live, for it is the form and distribution of the islands which have helped to produce the fauna which is now to be seen there.

The principal island, Mahé, has a land area of fifty-three square miles, and is the home of about 45,000 of the present human population of nearly 55,000 people. The two other large inhabited islands, Praslin and La Digue, thirty miles away, are respectively about twenty and two square miles in extent, with populations of some 3,000 and 1,000 people. La Digue is the most densely populated island in the group. A fourth large island, Silhouette, which has an area hardly less than that of La Digue, is privately owned, and has a population of about 500 people. Silhouette is very mountainous, with a peak at Morne Dauban over 2,500 feet, second only to the 3,000 feet peak of Mahé at Morne Seychellois. Praslin and La Digue, although they have steep hills, are less than 1,500 feet high.

Mahé and Silhouette have extensive areas of mountain forest above 1,500 feet, some of it undisturbed, especially on Silhouette, where the moss forest of Morne Dauban and the palms of Mt Cocos Marrons are of especial interest. Morne Seychellois on Mahé bears a unique cloud-forest: here, as well as in the forests of Silhouette, there are endemic populations of tree-frogs and chameleons, with snails and beetles which are found nowhere else. Although Praslin is lower, it, too, has a unique environment: the beautiful Vallée de Mai Nature Reserve, with its stands of Coco de Mer and other endemic palms, and its own unique fauna, including the Black Parrot. Much of the rest of central Praslin, and all of Curieuse, is forestry land owned by the Government. There are also large forestry tracts on Mahé.

The smaller islands have their own character. Some are intensively cultivated, especially Frigate with its citrus plantations and Marianne and Félicité, which are almost entirely under coconuts. Others, such as Aride, Cousin and Cousine, have rocky hills which defy cultivation; covered in bracken and small trees, these are the breeding places of large numbers of sea birds, as well as a few rare endemic land birds. The small areas of sea-level plateau on the small islands are uniformly under coconuts, with small groves of fruit trees and vegetable gardens.

The plateau on the larger islands is for the most part divided into estates, which grow coconuts, as well as other crops such as vanilla, cinnamon, and patchouli. The cinnamon, introduced by the early French settlers, has naturalised rather too successfully, especially on Mahé, where the lower foothills are extensively covered in thickets of these sturdy trees, regularly cropped for bark and leaves.

At the lower levels there is little left of the impenetrable forests which the settlers found when they first came. Only in parts of Silhouette and in a very few small patches on La Digue is there any lowland forest left; and of the once extensive mangrove swamps only small areas, such as Port Glaud and Barbarons, Mahé, and L'Amitié, Praslin, remain.

Higher in the hills of Mahé, cultivation is still dominant in most places, even up to the tea plantations above 1,500 feet. But in a few areas, notably Morne Blanc and Baton Rouge, the forest persists in gigantic splendour, along with much of its wild life. On Silhouette there is more such forest, and on Praslin some of the forestry land is preserved in or near its original condition. Higher still on Mahé and Silhouette, as we have seen, there is more of the original forest.

The influence of man on the habitats of Seychelles has thus seeped upwards from sea level, affecting the entire coastline to some extent: the higher one climbs into the hills the less marked the human interference, until one stands on the crest of Mahé or Silhouette in ancient forests, virtually unchanged. The barrier to new building above 1,200 feet, recently approved by Government, should have a valuable effect in preserving these glorious heights.

In summary, there are five main habitat types in Seychelles:

1 Sea level coastal Mangroves, *Scaevola*, *Guettarda*, Takamaka, *Casuarina*. Typically a beach crest bush with clearings round *Casuarina* and in creeks of mangrove swamps; now survives only in a few places in this form, but seen in attenuated form along the edges of plantations, where *Casuarina* is often planted as a windbreak among naturally occurring hedges of *Scaevola*.

Typical Birds: Herons nesting in mangroves, feeding in shallows. Fodies and sunbirds in bushes; mynahs and Ground Doves common on the beach down to the tide line.

2 Lowland plateau Badamier/Takamaka forest, largely replaced by coconut palms and other cultivation. The forest typically rather open, with deep damp leaf litter, fairly dense underbrush. *Pisonia* and *Morinda* now rare except on small islands, e.g. Cousin. Coconut plantations usually cleared of brush beneath palms, with small herbs forming thick mat.

Typical Birds: Fodies, sunbirds, kestrel; waxbill, lovebird in grassy clearings; mynah usually in open; swiftlet over wet places, moorhen in pools with reed cover.

3 Foothill forest (say 500 to 1,000 feet) Bois rouge, jackfruit, some albizzia in fairly dense forest with thick undergrowth. Replaced in most areas, especially on Mahé, with cinnamon thickets, and coco-plum on deforested hillsides. Much housing at this level.

Typical birds: kestrel, Blue Pigeon, Turtle Doves, bulbuls, sunbirds. Fodies less common; swiftlet occasional over trees.

4 Mountain forest (up to 2,000 feet) Denser and wetter than in the foothills, less undergrowth. Albizzia dominant, giant trees common, Wide assortment of other trees, mostly endemic; bois de beurre, bois rouge, bois dure, etc. Tree ferns, native palms, orchids, not uncommon. On open 'glacis' pitcher plants may be seen. Displaced by tea in central Mahé.

Typical birds: Blue Pigeon, Turtle Dove, white-eyes, sunbirds, bulbul. Mynah and kestrel rare except round habitation. Scops Owl now restricted to this level, nesting place of swiftlet, tropicbirds.

Note. On Praslin at this height the forest is dominated in the natural condition by endemic palms; on Silhouette the same is true, save that on the slopes of Morne Dauban the forest is more like that on Mahé. Evidently where there is nothing above the forest at 2,000 feet it develops into a palm forest; but the palms cannot compete with plants which colonise the hillsides above 2,000 feet, producing their own typical forest below. In the palm forest on Praslin the Black Parrot is the typical bird, with bulbuls and sunbirds common; on Silhouette in the same habitat there seems to be no parrot.

5 Moss forest (above 2,000 feet) Almost continuous cloud cover, tree ferns and mosses among bois noir, bois dure, some bois rouge. Little undergrowth, but many epiphytes. Tree frogs common.

Typical Birds: very few. Occasional white-eyes and sunbirds in clearings, Blue Pigeon and bulbul also seen. Too cool and damp for nesting in the forest proper, but clearings sometimes have a few pigeons.

Although the islands are small in area, they include in a limited space a wide variety of habitats from sea shore to high wet forest; this variety provides niches for a wider range of bird life than might perhaps have been expected from the map. The basic difference between the high islands, Mahé and Silhouette, and the lower mountainous islands, Praslin and La Digue, is that the latter tend to have the summits covered in palms rather than in hardwood forest. This might explain the distribution of certain bird species, notably the Black Parrot, never recorded from Mahé, and the high-forest white-eyes, never recorded anywhere but Mahé and Marianne. On this hypothesis, we should expect to find both species on Silhouette, the parrot at Mt Cocos Marrons in the palm forest, and white-eyes in the high forest of Morne Dauban; but neither has ever been seen there. Perhaps the areas are too small, or perhaps they are simply insufficiently explored.

The first impression of Seychelles, based on one's arrival in Victoria, and perhaps a journey across La Misère or over to Beauvallon, might suggest that there is nothing to be seen save pantropical vegetation and introduced birds – and some rather curious houses – but this is not really the case. Considering the small size of the islands, and the rapid growth of the population, it is remarkable how much unique and fascinating habitat is left: it is well worth the effort of going out of one's way to find it.

The next section concentrates on the historical changes in the fauna and flora of Seychelles. Since to the ecologist all changes must be for the worse when the original is altered, it might seem to be rather gloomy reading. The antidote to this is a walk in the mountain forest, perhaps along the Forêt Noire Road, or above the tea plantation at Morne Blanc, where all the surviving endemic birds of Mahé may still be seen.

Ornithological History

Before man stepped ashore, Seychelles was a piece of the distant past, preserved by a moat a thousand miles wide from the changes which had swept through the rest of the world. The islands were covered in impenetrable forests, in which flocks of birds shared their supremacy with giant tortoises and little lizards. Crocodiles lurked in the plateau lagoons. In Seychelles the reptiles maintained the position of superiority which they had lost almost everywhere else. Apart from the huge seacows basking round the shores, the only other mammals were two unique species of bats.

After a few years of settlement, however, the seacow was gone, just a folk memory preserved in the names of places like Ile aux Vaches, off Grand'Anse Mahé. The crocodile was no more, wiped out by the first settlers in a frenzy of terror: now it, too, is commemorated only by a few place names, and in the Créole word for a horsefly – *caiman*. Other changes in the fauna have been going on since the settlers arrived, including the almost total extermination of the giant tortoise. In this chapter I shall consider the extinctions and introductions which have modified the original bird fauna to produce the one described in this book.

The first permanent settlement in Seychelles was in 1770, consisting of twenty-seven people on Ste Anne Island. Four years later there were over 1,000 residents, mostly slaves, there and on Mahé, collecting coconuts as well as supplying tortoises and timber to passing ships and digging out the small stocks of guano. During the clearing of forests to establish the plantations, fires were a common occurrence, so that more land was cleared than was needed to grow the crops; the destruction of the islands had started. In 1788 de Malavois mentioned the Waxbill as one of the most common birds of Mahé; the contamination of the endemic avifauna by the introduction of alien species was also under way.

Clearance continued as the population grew. There were 1,820 residents in 1802, growing coconuts and cotton where the lowland forests once stood. A century later, in 1906, Michael Nicoll saw rubber being planted at Cascade, where there were already stands of cocoa and cashew; cinnamon had got out of hand and was naturalised, growing vigorously right to the top of the smaller mountains. To the present day the clearance goes on, felling the forests to plant other things in their place: tea in the central highlands, radio aerials at La Misère, and little houses practically everywhere. The remains of the endemic forest, principally on the slopes of Morne Seychellois and on Silhouette, are now protected, hopefully not too late for their survival.

Praslin suffered appallingly from fires and clearing during the eighteenth century and thereafter, but by a miracle some Cocos de Mer survived in the Vallée de Mai, and a few Black Parrots with them to repopulate the island. Silhouette has also had its fires, but there are tracts of endemic forest surviving there, too, including the beautiful stand on Morne Dauban, though there seem to be very few birds of any interest. La Digue retains some endemic woodland among the coconut palms, and in it the Veuve, one of the typical species of this habitat. On other islands tiny remnants of the endemic bird species survive: the Magpie Robin on Frigate, the Brush Warbler on Cousin, and the Seychelles Fody on both. Considering the tale of destruction, it is surprising that only two of the original land birds became extinct (as far as we know) – the Green Parakeet, *Psittacula eupatria wardi*, and the Chestnut-flanked White-eye, *Zosterops mayottensis semiflava*, both in about 1900.

The seabirds have suffered less conspicuously but no less finally: the Great Frigate is now very rare or extinct as a breeding species in the central group of islands, and the Red-footed Booby is extinct. Both these species nested in large tame colonies, and both were raided and finally wiped out to provide food and bait for fishing. The egg-collecting 'industry' has decimated the

Sooty Tern on some islands, and seriously reduced the Common
Noddy. The cropping of the chicks of the Wedge-tailed Shearwater and the White-tailed Tropicbird for salting as delicacies
still goes on on some small islands, but on Cousin and Aride it
has been stopped, possibly in time to prevent permanent damage
to the species. Adults and chicks of the tropicbirds and Audubon's
Shearwater, and even tiny birds such as the Fairy Tern, have
been slaughtered to provide a change of diet.

The dodo became extinct because it was easy to catch:
ironically, it was not even good to eat. If Seychelles had had a
similar bird it would have suffered the same fate, but so far as
we can discover there was no such flightless bird here. The only
species among the land birds which have been reduced for food
seem to have been the Blue Pigeon and the Turtle Dove. In
1906 Nicoll saw large flocks of Blue Pigeon at Cascade, where
the owner regarded them as an edible asset; now, thanks to
shooting and predation by the Barn Owl, they are a rare sight
on Mahé except in the higher forest, and scarcely more common
on Praslin and the few other islands where they survive.

Other species were attacked by the settlers and their successors
because they were considered to be pests. The beautiful little
Seychelles Kestrel suffered because it took chicks from the
settlers' yards; rather than cover their runs they killed kestrels.
Also this unfortunate species is regarded as a bird of ill omen,
and it may still be killed simply for approaching too close to a
house. The Black Parrot, very numerous on Praslin in the old
days, must have been a menace to fruit-growers: flocks of over
a hundred birds were seen on mango trees, stripping the crop as
it ripened, and one can understand the feelings of the trees'
owners, who shot the parrots. They succeeded almost too well,
and with the support of the forest clearance men and fires they
nearly extinguished the species.

These three species of land bird were reduced by the deliberate
efforts of men; but other species were destroyed by accident,
through changes in the environment, and through the introduction of predators and competitive species. I have already
described the destruction of the habitat; in such disturbed times

as those, the added effect of mammalian predators such as cats and rats, on a bird population which had evolved to live with nothing more dangerous to it than a large lizard, must have been terrific. At any rate, we can see the results now. Only two species of land bird seem to have lived through these changes undisturbed: the sunbird and the swiftlet. One might hazard the guess that both were too specialised to be affected by the competition of such alien species as arrived, yet versatile enough to live on in the rapidly changing environment. In addition, both have nests which are inaccessible to rats.

The Green Parakeet was said to be 'nearly exterminated' in 1866, because it attacked maize crops, and evidently the job was completed soon afterwards. The Chestnut-flanked White-eye probably suffered extinction from the loss of its habitat. A little less lucky or resilient than the others, these species are now to be seen only as skins in museums.

ADDITIONS

Birds which colonise islands have to overcome certain difficulties if they are to survive. These difficulties and the means of overcoming them are described in another chapter, and there is a magnificent account of island birds in Sherwin Carlquist's book, *Island Life*. Basically, the points are these:

1. Any species inhabiting an island must have crossed the barrier of alien habitat with which the island is surrounded, and have arrived in sufficient numbers to start a breeding group. This limits the number of species found on an undisturbed island, producing an 'open ecosystem' with vacant niches. Strongly flighted birds may visit islands without colonising them, or they may incorporate them into their breeding range without the local population becoming isolated. The most frequently isolated colonists are weak fliers, such as rails and white-eyes, which get blown to the islands by storms and cannot get away again.

2. Island birds tend to have generalised feeding habits, and they

take time to acquire the habit of commensalism with man. Thus when a newly populated island is invaded by man's pets and pests, the invaders can often flourish with little or no competition from the residents, and usually to their detriment.

3. Because islands are sharply delimited, there can be no tapering off of the population of birds at their edges. This tends to produce a lowered breeding rate among insular birds, which are therefore often swamped numerically by invaders from the continents, with a higher breeding rate.

The bird fauna of a typical remote island will thus consist of few species, usually only one from each family of successful colonists. Long distance fliers such as swifts and pigeons, flocking birds such as parrots and white-eyes, and long-lived birds such as owls and kestrels, are best able to solve the transport problem. Adaptable birds such as finches (weavers), sunbirds, thrushes (magpie robins), and bulbuls will be able to make best use of a strange environment once the initial invasion has succeeded. Other types, such as flycatchers and warblers, arrive by chance, and chance alone decides whether they survive. Thus the distribution of these last groups among the islands of the world is discontinuous and apparently illogical. Rollers and cuckoos are frequent arrivals in Seychelles, but so far none has managed to colonise the islands. Most of them are too battered to breed by the time storm winds have thrown them on to the islands.

Introductions by man cut across this pattern by artificially solving the transport problem, and sometimes by ensuring deliberately that enough of the species are transported to enable them to start breeding. For example, the Indian Hill Mynah was introduced to Seychelles from Mauritius in the early nineteenth century, by Mahé de la Bourdonnais. It had been introduced into Mauritius in the first place to control locusts: as a fact, locusts are virtually unknown in Seychelles, but perhaps de la Bourdonnais didn't know that, or perhaps the mynah did its job very efficiently! Whether the mynah found any locusts or not, it increased abundantly on insects and fruit, lizards and assorted refuse, helped by the fact that it is an ancient commensal of man, able to live close by his habitations and to benefit from his by-products. Once the species was here, its rapid breeding rate enabled it to swamp any competition, until now it is the most abundant bird in the lowlands.

The cardinal was introduced at about the same time, succeeding in displacing an earlier seed-eating introduction, the African Waxbill. Although it is a Malagasy bird, the cardinal was common on Mauritius in very early days. Despite popular belief, it is unlikely that it displaced the endemic weaver, the Toq Toq. The waxbill is now rare except in certain parts of south Mahé, and on La Digue, where it is locally common. The Ground Dove was brought in by the same route as the mynah, from India via Mauritius, I suppose because it is such a pretty little thing to have around the house. These three, the mynah, the cardinal, and the Barred Ground Dove, are the most common land birds in Seychelles, and between them they make up almost the whole of the avifauna of the coastal plateau of Mahé and Praslin.

If a bird species cannot displace the endemic form, it may be able to infiltrate it. This is what happened between the introduced Malagasy Turtle Dove and the Seychelles Turtle Dove, which is a subspecies of the former. The two races have now interbred to such an extent that they can be distinguished only on Cousin and Cousine, and even there there are many hybrid individuals. C. W. Benson suggests that the Malagasy subspecies arrived in Diego Garcia as surplus food stores on some early pirate ship; and it is reasonable to suppose that they got to Seychelles in the same way. They could hardly have made the journey without human assistance – or if they did, it is a huge coincidence that they arrived so soon after the first human colonists. They were probably helped to establish themselves by the fact that the endemic subspecies was rare at least on Mahé when they arrived. Although this particular introduction has not made a radical difference to the appearance of the birds of Seychelles, it is one which causes great grief to ornithologists, who would have delighted in the comparisons and contrasts to be found in such widely separated populations of the same species.

The most recent introduction has perhaps been the most catastrophic. In 1949, and again in 1951 and 1952, the Department of Agriculture imported East African Barn Owls and liberated them in order to control rats. As one might have predicted even at the time, they were unable to catch rats in the unfamiliar habitat – in fact they died out on Ile Platte, where they were first introduced, and Platte is infested with rats – and they have turned their attention to birds. The Fairy Tern has been all but wiped out on Mahé and Praslin by the owl, and many other species have suffered, including the kestrel, which has been ousted from its nesting sites among the rocks and in church towers. One priest told me that he prefers to have owls in his tower; they make less noise during services. There is now a bounty of Rs.30 on the Barn Owl, but it will be a long time even at that price before it is brought under control. Meanwhile, the rats are being attacked with poison.

The Grey-headed Lovebird was introduced at the turn of the century, and for some years it was very common all over Mahé, with huge roosting flocks in Gordon Square in the nineteen thirties; then, quite suddenly, it became scarce, until now lovebirds are to be seen only in a few places in West Mahé, and on Silhouette, where they were artificially introduced.

These changes in the original unspoilt bird life of Seychelles were for the most part inevitable, and there is no point in mourning them. As always with the delicate balance of ecology, once the mistake is made there is no second chance. Man mars wherever he puts his foot ashore. We cannot hope to restore the original state; but we can decide to preserve jealously whatever little we have left.

All the land birds of Seychelles are protected by law, most of them since 1906 – when, not coincidentally, Lord Crawford visited the islands. But all the laws in the world cannot ensure the survival of one bird without public support; and the only hope for the birds of Seychelles is the education of the people. This is proceeding, as they come to realise the value of their unique avifauna, not only to themselves and their tourist industry, but to the world at large.

FUTURE TRENDS

Prediction is dangerous, especially in a book, but it is a temptation hard to resist, so I shall take the risk.

Victoria and its environs are spreading fast, as new building techniques enable people to indulge their taste for living high up, and as the population of traders and leisured people increases. New estates on both sides of the La Misère Pass are joining with the town below and the Tracking Station above to create a strip of suburbia right across the mountains, where the primary and more recently the secondary forests once stood. Areas which in 1965 I could hardly penetrate on hands and knees, in search of white-eyes and Scops Owls, are now accessible by saloon car over rapidly improving and extending roads. As this settlement of the higher slopes continues, here and elsewhere on Mahé, the remaining mountain forest is being eroded away until there is a danger that only the reserves and a few catchment areas will be left undisturbed. These might be big enough to shelter some of the characteristic plants of higher altitudes, but whether they will be able to support a breeding population of the rare mountain birds is open to doubt.

On other islands the situation is equally uncertain. On Frigate the least further development could endanger the Magpie Robin, at present apparently recovering now that feral cats have nearly been wiped out on the island. On La Digue the flycatcher is at the point of extinction. One or both of these populations might have passed the minimum figure for permanent recovery. On Praslin the principal habitat of the Black Parrot is protected now, and it shelters also bulbuls, Blue Pigeon, and sunbirds; the situation here looks more promising, and there is reason to hope that the present very small populations of parrots and pigeons might recover in time.

The development of the tourist industry will place a tremendous strain on the ecology of the whole archipelago: there must be an increase in housing and other amenities, as well as more intensive and extensive cultivation, to provide food for the hotels, and perhaps to take advantage of the airmail market for tropical delicacies. Careful control over the importation of fruits, flowers, and animals, and their passenger parasites, will help to prevent disasters of introduction such as have happened in the past. Above all, the development of reserves and National Parks will protect what is left of the islands' unique wildlife, while making it more accessible even to the less athletic visitor.

The Outer Islands – Aldabra and the Amirantes

The islands included in the scope of this book, apart from central Seychelles, are the Aldabras (Assumption, Cosmoledo, Astove, and Aldabra itself); the Amirantes, from African Islands in the north to S. François in the south; and Providence, Farquhar, and St Pierre, which are seldom visited save by local workers.

These islands have several factors in common which distinguish them from the high islands of central Seychelles. They are all low, rising to little more than sixty feet, and that only where there are tall sand dunes; most of them had substantial deposits of guano, seabird fertiliser, nearly completely dug out now; and they all have a water shortage, depending on irregular rainfall. They are all atolls or parts of atolls; that is, they were formed by the growth of coral on a shallow submarine bank, usually with sand washed up against it. In the strange case of Aldabra and St Pierre the old coral has been raised above the sea surface to form a land surface of hard limestone rock.

The islands were probably located by the Portuguese during their age of exploration in the sixteenth and seventeenth centuries, but because of the shortage of water none of them was inhabited until long after the settlement of Seychelles in 1770. The Amirantes were the first to be colonised, by planters of coconuts in the mid-nineteenth century, and once a supply of water had been assured by building catchment tanks, they must have been idyllic places to live; indeed they still are.

The Amirantes are low coral atolls, hardly raised above sea level, protected from inundation by their fringing reefs. Navigation among them is a job for experts – even some local skippers will not venture among them at night. All the islands are now covered with coconuts, with the exception of Desnoeufs, the egg island, where despite the heavy cropping which still continues there are upwards of a million pairs of Sooty Terns in the

biggest colony in these waters. There are very few land birds in
the Amirantes now, though there was at one time an endemic
Turtle Dove to our knowledge, and there may have been other
unique forms. Now, however, the land birds are introductions from
Seychelles or elsewhere: cardinals and sparrows predominate,
with occasional oddities such as the Indian Francolin, presumably
introduced as a sporting bird. The surviving Turtle Doves have
hybridised with the Malagasy form.

Where the Amirantes excel is in their seabird colonies: the
little-visited parts of the larger atolls bear breeding colonies of
boobies, shearwaters, and terns of several species. On African
Banks in particular the terns and herons breed in large numbers,
virtually undisturbed by visitors.

The pattern of development has been very similar throughout
the group: where guano was present it was soon dug out and
exported, and, with the loss of the forests which it used to support,
the birds which produced the resource in the first place simply
died out, or moved elsewhere. The forests must have contained
Pisonia and *Morinda*, with fringes of *Guettarda* and *Scaevola*, and
occasional *Siuriana* and *Callophyllum* (Takamaka) at the beach
crest. Once they were gone, the way was open for the planting
of palms and *Casuarina*, both important cash crops in those days.
Where there was little or no guano, the palms were planted
straight away: and as soon as they were planted, the islands
began to run down – they lost their ecological diversity, which
was never very great in the first place, and became the home of
weeds and pests. (Pets, which accompany man wherever he
wanders, very soon acquire the extra 's' on islands where mammals
have never been before.)

The Farquhar Group, Providence, Cerf, and Farquhar itself,
are very similar to their neighbours the Amirantes. They suffered
the same fate, and although they are now very beautiful to the
eye of the city-weary wanderer from the northern hemisphere,
they are relatively barren to the ecologist. There is an old
record, dated 1821, of a small Blue Pigeon on St Pierre and
Providence, but no one has seen it since then, and it is surely
extinct from the islands. Their seabird life has survived, however,

rather as it has in the Amirantes, in parts of the islands where it has not come under pressure.

The island of St Pierre, which lies nearer to Farquhar than to anywhere else, once had a particularly rich deposit of guano – with the result that it attracted more attention from the miners than the other islands in the area. Where once it was covered with dense forests of *Pisonia*, most of its surface is now bare rock, pitted where the last ounce of phosphate has been scraped off. In the very centre of the island there is a single *Pisonia* tree, stunted and twisted; and the birds have gone. This makes the birdman gnash his teeth more than you might think: for St Pierre is a raised atoll very like Aldabra, but it differed in being covered in tall forests; now that they and their birds have gone, the chance of comparing two neighbouring examples of this rare type of island has gone too.

Aldabra itself has become famous as the result of the protests which were raised when the military wanted to build an air base on the atoll. Before this, however, the group had been visited only by a few travellers, of which I was myself one. Much as I treasure my memories of visiting the island before the world knew of its existence, I cannot but rejoice at the wealth of information which has come out of it since the Royal Society started work there. The importance of the atoll scientifically has been proved beyond doubt.

Aldabra was known to the Arabs before the Portuguese found it; indeed its name is thought to be a corruption of an Arab word meaning 'green'. It lay near the route between Arabia and Zanzibar, and probably several navigators were washed by storms on to its jagged shores. So inhospitable is it, though, that no attempt was made to colonise it until 1888, when the first lease was taken out by one Jules Cauvin of Mahé. The island had been raided for Giant Tortoises before then, and there must have been a few temporary camps there, but Cauvin's was the first settlement in the true sense. Since that time, with a short break during and after the Second World War, there has been some kind of human settlement on the island, numbering seldom as many as one hundred people.

The other islands in the Aldabra group were colonised at about the same time, but they suffered more drastically than Aldabra ever did. Their trouble was that, like St Pierre, they had large accessible deposits of guano. Assumption was the last to be settled, in 1908, but it was the first to be rendered almost entirely barren of wild life, and Cosmoledo was not far behind. Astove, too, was heavily mined, but not quite to the extent of Assumption and Cosmoledo, and consequently there is more there to see to-day than at either of the others.

There is one exception to this wholesale dismissal of Assumption and Cosmoledo as places to visit: that is South Island, Cosmoledo. When Michael Nicoll visited the island in 1906, it had a flightless rail and a turtle dove of its own – but it has seldom if ever been visited since then, certainly not by an ornithologist. There just might be a relict population there of birds which are extinct elsewhere; or there might be nothing.

Aldabra itself already has another book, Tony Beamish's account of his visit there in 1966. There is also the vast volume produced by the first three parts of the Royal Society Expedition (*Philosophical Transactions of the Royal Society of London*, Vol. 260). Both these cover the bird life to some extent, Beamish giving a traveller's view of the birds supplemented by an admirable taxonomic list by Bill Bourne, and the Royal Society taking detailed note of each species in a complete technical account – which I helped to write. This latter is probably more than the average visitor would want to know, and certainly more than he would want to carry – the volume is the size of a telephone directory. Thus in this book I shall give field notes and some taxonomic information to complete the account by Tony Beamish – those who want more can seek out the directory.

The habitat on the low coral atolls, for all their lack of rainfall, is lush and fairly moist, partly because of the abundance there of beach vegetation, and partly because of the proximity of the warm lagoon. The complete cover of coconuts helps, too. On Aldabra it is quite different. The land surface is larger than on the other islands, so that one can get farther away from the sea; but because the land is raised, there is a lens of fresh water floating on salt water in the porous rock, with the result that here and there there are freshwater pools, in and around which there is a unique Aldabran freshwater inland habitat. In places where the rock is impermeable, the water evaporates very quickly without contributing to the lens, and here the surface is barren and bare, with only occasional hardy shrubs surviving in the baking heat. In places like this one can begin to understand what dehydration means. But over most of the atoll the rock surface is dissected into spikes and pinnacles, so that the water runs straight through, eventually contributing to the lens. Here deep pits with razor edges contain salt or brackish water, and the whole surface is covered in a hellish shrub called *Pemphis acidula,* wiry of stem, and almost impossible to cut. This combination of jagged rock and impenetrable bush is what has protected Aldabra in the past, quite apart from the lack of drinking water. The locals call this type of fossil coral 'champignon' because where it outcrops in the lagoon it is typically weathered away by the tide to form mushroom-shaped islets.

Living in this rugged and rather harsh environment are twelve forms of land bird which are unique to the atoll, including the White-throated Rail, the last surviving flightless bird in the Indian Ocean. Only two of these forms are endemic full species, the Brush Warbler and the Drongo; the rest are subspecies of birds which occur also in Madagascar and elsewhere. Although their isolation on Aldabra has not been long enough or complete enough to cause their evolution into distinct species, the birds of Aldabra are of great interest, partly because the Aldabran environment is so free from interference by man. It is still possible to walk in parts of Aldabra where man has never trodden before, and to see birds innocent of fear. The tamest of all is the rail, which will investigate one's clothing and walk over one's feet, blissfully ignorant of the fate of those of its neighbours which have abandoned flight in security. Another especially fearless inhabitant is the Sacred Ibis, a distinct subspecies, whose juveniles in particular show unabated curiosity.

Perhaps the greatest attraction of Aldabra to the passing ornithologist is the huge colonies of seabirds, especially the frigates and boobies. Swarming like mosquitoes above their mangrove homes, the Great and Lesser Frigates present a spectacle which has to be seen to be half-believed; and their neighbours the boobies, for all their uncomplimentary name, are beautiful by contrast with the angular and bony frigates.

All this bird life is hardly altered at all by man's scratching about on Aldabra. True, there are fewer birds to be seen on Settlement Island than elsewhere, but on the whole atoll there is no introduced species – although the Pied Crow and the kestrel may both have arrived since man came, being dependent on him for food and nest sites (in planted coconut palms) respectively.

The human history of Aldabra is a fascinating study, with traces of a few attempts to found a settlement before the present site was chosen; but even with tortoise raids and mangrove-cutting, it is irrelevant. The impact of man on the atoll as a whole has been negligible. Darwin wrote to the Governor of Mauritius in 1874, warning him of the danger to the tortoises and the rest of the Aldabran fauna if the island were exploited; but although his warning was disregarded the wildlife has survived, protected by the sheer inhospitality of the island. The Hon. Walter Rothschild paid half the rent of Aldabra for some years on condition that the lessee protected the tortoises, but the real protection came from the fact that it was physically impossible to exploit the tortoises completely – not, of course, to belittle the value of the gesture.

Now, barring some unforeseen military emergency – for the option to build a base on Aldabra is still open to the Americans as well as to the British – the island is safe, a refuge for rare birds and animals whose relatives elsewhere have been destroyed.

The Ecological Importance of Islands

Ecology involves the study of all aspects of the environment: not only the soil, the vegetation, and the animal life, but also man, and all their interactions. It is not something that happens only in Nature Reserves. There is much of great importance to be learned from the ecology of city parks and indeed city pavements, as well as from National Parks and the bed of the sea. So much of the surface of the developed countries is now suburban if not urban development that the former studies might in some ways be more important. Not long ago the members of London's Stock Exchange were scratching their shrewd heads and wondering what to do about the invasion of their new building by hordes of mice. There is no doubt that we need to learn to understand the ways of other animals before we can control their lives.

No factor in ecology is too small to consider, including the effect of modern temperature-regulating equipment on the breeding rate of mice fed on left-over sandwiches. The well-known food chain or food web might seem simple enough to understand or even control, but a small change in one component can have far-reaching effects. We have seen an example of this recently in the matter of the Crown of Thorns Starfish on the Great Barrier Reef. Ecological balances are often on a knife edge, and it needs only a slight interference with the balance to cause violent upsets.

Interdependence is the keynote of ecology. It is sometimes not realised that prey species need not suffer from the attentions of predators, for example, and that this could include the Sooty Tern and its egg-predator man, if only the predation could be kept at an ecologically viable level. Unfortunately, the structure of the web of interdependence is so complex and delicately adjusted as to make it virtually impossible to recreate once it has been damaged. Even if the component species exist elsewhere, to fit them into the system so that it will balance again requires detailed knowledge which was almost certainly not collected before the system was damaged. One sees why conservationists sometimes get so discouraged, and why some of them become ardent preservationists instead, advocating the exclusion of man from wild places.

We may hope, however, that man is going to be around for a long time to come, and in more and more of the once remote places. He has to try to find a way of sharing his existence with wild things and wild places in such a way that both benefit. This needs extensive and serious study, because we are fast approaching the point at which our entire environment is man-made. Indeed, for those who live in the great cities this is already true. The wilderness, if they ever find it, may be more than a day's journey away from their daily sphere.

Islands are important in this for two reasons: first because one or two of them are still practically uncontaminated (though – or because – they are difficult to find), and second because much of the remaining wilderness is in the form of islands – islands of jungle or prairie or moorland in a sea of man. For these reasons it is essential that we should study wild places such as parts of Seychelles and Aldabra, not only for the sake of people who will appreciate their glories in days to come, but for the application of the knowledge we gain here to insular situations elsewhere.

INVASION AND COLONISATION

The animals on an island are either a relict population, left behind when the island was cut off from the mainland, or they have invaded the island by crossing the barrier that divides it from the mainland – or they may be a combination of both. In the following discussion about Seychelles I shall try to keep to considerations of birds, and I shall assume that they all got here by invasion, which seems most likely, if not certain. The age of Seychelles is not properly known, but it seems probable that the islands are too old to have had a relict population of birds when they were cut off.

Birds capable of crossing the ocean are more numerous than one might at first think. Obviously the larger species can fly across, but even tiny birds have made the journey, assisted by wind, travelling over 1,000 miles and arriving in a fit state to breed. Huge tree trunks are sometimes seen drifting at sea; when they are washed up they disembark insects, snails, frogs, and even small birds, but seldom even the smallest mammals. I have seen a clump of bamboo washed up on the coast of Aldabra in which the stems were fully a foot in diameter and about a hundred in number; such a floating island must have had thousands of passengers, both animals and plants, travelling in relative safety and comfort in its hollow stems.

Some groups of birds are better than others at crossing the barrier. Examples of good invaders represented in Seychelles are the white-eyes, sunbirds, and fodies. Others are quite frequent arrivals, too, for example rollers and cuckoos and certain birds of prey. Birds such as wheatears and bee-eaters turn up here more or less regularly, but they must be classed as poor invaders, or vagrants. The true migrants, such as waders, come here regularly but return to their summer quarters to breed. They are not invaders in the strict sense, though there is some evidence that one of them, the Greater Sandplover, *Charadrius leschenaultii*, may have bred as far south as Somalia as well as in its usual breeding grounds in north-east Europe.

The number of different invading species which an island group can collect is determined largely by its distance from continents and its size. Seychelles, being small even in the old days when more land was exposed than now, and isolated by more than 600 miles from Madagascar, has a rather small avifauna – though botanically it is richer than would be expected, and this is not readily explained.

Successful colonisation as opposed to mere invasion demands more from the birds. If they are to settle and breed on an island they must first fulfil certain conditions. First, at least a male and female in breeding condition must arrive unscathed. This means that the flocking birds such as white-eyes have a distinct advantage, because it is likely that several will arrive at once. Solitary birds such as cuckoos (which in addition have specialised breeding habits) obviously have a bad start, and tend to be unsuccessful in colonisation. In the same way, long-lived birds are better adapted to wait for the arrival of a mate than birds with a shorter life span; this is where owls and kestrels have an advantage.

The second demand to be satisfied for successful colonisation is that the birds should be adaptable, so that they can make the best of the alien environment when they arrive. Birds whose feeding or nesting requirements are too specialised are unlikely to survive.

The third condition is rather more difficult to understand: there must be enough invaders to give rise to a viable population. This rather nebulous 'mystic number' has been studied by MacArthur and Wilson (1967), who call it a 'propagule'. The discussion in their book is rather mathematical; basically, the propagule is that number of a species below which colonisation will fail although there may be some initial breeding success. The reason for failure might be genetic, with certain species more prone than others to failure through inbreeding, or it might be simply logistic, with the sexes not meeting often enough to ensure at least one encounter per season when both are in breeding condition. Perhaps the Grey-headed Lovebird is an example of genetic failure in Seychelles, where the original half-dozen bred with tremendous success for thirty years, and then declined to become rare.

With survivors, as with invaders, the population may be too small to exist for long. We do not know whether we have reached the point of failure yet with any of the declining species in Seychelles; but that is typical of this type of extinction. Whales in the Arctic and tigers in Bengal have both probably reached the point of no return, but imperceptibly. Only when we come to realise their value and start to watch their numbers do we realise that such species are doomed. Possibly the Paradise Flycatcher and the Scops Owl could both reach this point soon, if they haven't already.

LIMITING FACTORS

Certain features of the island may restrict the population of a bird species below the level for continued survival. The commonest of these is the lack of fresh water, which probably explains why there are so few breeding land birds in the Amirantes, for example. If sufficient fresh water is available, space is the next essential need: there are very many islands which support only sea birds because there is not room for enough land birds to hold the territories which are essential for breeding. Food is usually not limiting on islands; insects and flowering plants are among the best colonisers, so that there is food enough for most tastes, given that the space on the island is sufficient. The larger an island is, the more varied it will tend to be, and the more species it will support, depending also on its distance from the source of colonisation. Aldabra, although it is farthest of the group from Madagascar, has many more forms of bird because it is the largest island. The birds almost certainly used the other islands as 'stepping stones' on their way to Aldabra, but were unable to survive for long in the restricted range of habitat there.

Islands must experience many colonisations and extinctions over the ages. In this sense the bird population at any time is a stage in a continually changing process; but there are some species whose numbers, birth and death rate, age at first breeding, and other characters make it almost certain that they will survive indefinitely, and it is these species which comprise the 'permanent' population.

Even if the limiting factors permit the bird population to survive, they are bound to restrict its expansion beyond a certain level, nearly always that determined by the space available. The birds have evolved ways of raising this level, as we shall see shortly.

One way in which islands are less limiting than mainlands is in their relative lack of competition. On the continents such competition between species is important, leading to specialisation as the birds share out the resources between the species trying to use them. This leads to 'adaptive radiation', as can be seen in the tit and finch populations in European woodlands. On islands, on the other hand, the tendency is often in the other direction, with a lack of competition leading to generalisation, which has a marked effect on the evolutionary tendencies of the birds.

Evolutionary Tendencies of Island Life

The two main features of island life which affect the birds once they have colonised an island are the relatively high density of the population of their own species, and the relatively low level of competition from other species. In other and more epigrammatic words, the pressures of life on islands are more intraspecific than interspecific. On mainlands the two may be more nearly equal, or tending towards the interspecific. The effects of intraspecific competition on islands may be seen in the breeding rate, colour, and size of members of insular populations as compared with their mainland relatives.

BREEDING RATE

The colonising population expands until it is stopped by a limiting factor, probably space. At this point the birds have two choices open to them, so to speak; either they can continue to breed at the same rate, with large losses especially among the young, or they can change their breeding rate. (Now read that again, substituting 'man' for 'the birds'.) The latter is what usually happens, not of course from the choice of the birds, but from the operation of factors outside their control.

The increasing density of birds leads to an increase in the competition for space; territories become smaller under this pressure, so that the food for the nestlings is more difficult to find. Parents with large broods may have great difficulty in keeping all their chicks adequately nourished, with the result either that all the chicks die, or that the survivors are small and weakly compared with chicks from less numerous broods. It becomes quite possible that the birds which leave more descendants, those whose children produce the most grandchildren, are those which have a tendency to lay *smaller* clutches. Smaller clutches could produce stronger birds, which are more likely to breed successfully when their turn comes; and what's more, their offspring will inherit the tendency to smaller clutches, so that the normal clutch size for the species becomes smaller. Reduced clutch size in island birds as compared with their mainland relatives is often observed, and I think that this is the reason for it. For an example, the brush warblers on Madagascar lay clutches of four eggs; the recently discovered brush warbler on Aldabra had three; and the Seychelles Brush Warbler, probably though not certainly closely related, lays one egg or occasionally two. Let it be said here, however, that some biologists regard this theory as rank heresy.

Some birds retain large clutch sizes wherever they are, for example owls. In these birds the mechanism of population control is rather different: the eggs hatch at intervals in the order in which they were laid, not synchronously as in most birds, with the result that there are young in the nest of different ages. In times of food shortage, the smaller young are killed and eaten by the larger. This method has the advantage that it is adaptable to good conditions, producing more birds: clearly it would be a useful adaptation to a bird colonising new territory, such as the African Barn Owl in Seychelles.

The reduction in clutch size is advantageous in the island situation for as long as that situation is undisturbed: there are few dangers or predators. However, it leaves island birds open to rapid destruction by introduced predators, and it leaves them at a disadvantage compared with rapid-breeding competitive species introduced from the continents. Examples in Seychelles: the Barn Owl wipes out the Fairy Tern over a large part of its range within a very few years after being introduced; the mynah, already adapted to living with man, outbreeds the endemic bulbul in their competition for the resources of the lowland plateau, newly disturbed and invaded by man and his works.

COLOUR (AND TO SOME EXTENT SONG)

You will notice that the birds of Seychelles, beautiful though they may be, are drab or dark-coloured compared with those of the African or Indian mainland, even their close relatives. This can be linked with an insular life.

The drabness of island birds could be seen as another product of the limitation of territories resulting from high population density. The territories held by birds for the purpose of breeding are usually exclusive of all other birds of the same species, especially males, except the mate and the chicks. This means that other birds cannot usually feed or drink in the territory of a breeding pair, and when the species concerned breeds all the year round, as in the Seychelles Fody, this could constitute a severe limitation on the numbers which can live on an island.

There are two ways of overcoming this difficulty, both used by the fody here. The first, despite its tendency to close off areas to non-breeding birds, is continued breeding throughout the year. This seems paradoxical, but in fact continuous breeding means that parts of a territory can be used by several pairs during the course of a year, taking it in turns. The second method, which I want to examine in more detail, is a reduction in the brightness of the breeding dress, and in the colour of the species generally.

The suggestion is that if the breeding dress of the male is drab, and not too different from his off-season dress, he will be more easily able to invade the territory of another male to make use of its resources. Thus if a tree is fruiting abundantly in the territory of a breeding pair, drabber males will have a better chance of invading the territory to feed on the tree without provoking aggression from the territory's owner. Any reduction in aggression is advantageous to the individuals concerned, whether attacker or attacked, because it reduces their chances of getting hurt or killed in a fight. Dull or drab breeding dress also permits the establishment of places where the birds can congregate on a limited resource such as water, without excessive fighting between breeding males. This is not an absolute removal of conflict: breeding males will still challenge each other, and may even fight on occasion with great ferocity, but because the intensity of the breeding coloration is less, the amount and intensity of the fighting is also lower, and this reduction is sufficient to make life possible on the island for more birds.

The reduction of aggression is not the only possible explanation for the drabness of insular birds. Another is the reduced need for interspecific recognition signals on the island. On the mainland, the male at least has to show the flag in distinctive and often very bright colours if he is to attract females of his own species: and often the females select the most brightly marked males, keeping up the standard of the species by this means. Where there are a lot of closely related species one would expect to find the greatest and brightest variety of colour patterns, as for example among the sunbirds and starlings of Africa. On islands, however, the selection of males by females is not nearly so intense, since there is little or no risk of confusion between species; so the drabber males succeed in addition to the brighter, and the typical colour of the species becomes drabber. One objection to this theory is that if females stopped selecting males for their colour the result would be an avian King's Road, with a wild array of variations on the theme. However, although the females may not be selecting for the brightest any more, they are still recognising the basic pattern of the species; so that a sunbird which is golden all over will be unlikely to breed successfully. Further, it seems likely that the breeding dress in the mainland situation would, as I have suggested above, be the brightest possible for the species while separating it from other bright species, so that any departure from the mainland norm as sexual selection pressure was reduced would be in the direction of drabness.

As usual in biology, both these suggestions may be partly right, and they may be linked. If reduced sexual selection pressure started a trend towards drabber breeding dress, and then if the drabber birds survived better because they were not involved in so many fights, both trends would be in the same direction, and the result would be a population drabber than its mainland relatives.

The pressures tending towards drabness in Seychelles birds have not operated uniformly, however. The fody, the white-eye, the sunbird, the magpie robin, and even the swiftlet, have all followed the trend to drabness or dark colour to some extent, but the scops owl and the kestrel are both brighter than other members of their genera living nearby, and so were the extinct parakeet and white-eye. Perhaps in their case the drive to drabness was offset by the reduction of some other pressure, such as the need for camouflage.

The observed colour of birds is determined by pressures from their habitat and mode of life; apart from sexual selection, other factors such as crypticity, warning coloration, climate, and even diet all have their effect. When one of these pressures is relaxed, the colour patterns can develop until they are restrained once more by another pressure. The potential range of colours in birds is very wide; one has only to look at some of the grotesqueries produced by aviculturalists to see this. The tendency in island populations happens as a rule to be away from the spectacular.

Before leaving the subject of the effects of population density we ought to consider song, which is an aspect of display, if only to note that in many of the Seychelles birds whose relatives have strong songs on the mainland, for example, the fody and the magpie robin, the tendency to sing is reduced, and the song likewise subdued. Perhaps this is related to the reduction in the size of territories, like the drab plumage. The most accomplished singer in Seychelles is the Brush Warbler, which inconveniently defies the rule, since it has indeed drab plumage, but a marvellously variable and complex song.

SIZE AND ADAPTABILITY

The lack of competition from other species has given island birds the chance to use a wider range of resources than their ancestors could on the mainland. On the mainland, interspecific competition demands that birds become specialised, and in consequence that they should effectively waive their claim to that part of the food supply which other species are adapted to utilise. These adaptations are often in the size of bill required to cope with different sizes of prey. If the larger birds were removed from this situation, the smaller birds would not gain much at first, because of their very smallness; but if the smaller birds were removed, the larger birds could take over at least a part of their food supply, because within limits a large bill is more adaptable than a small one.

When a species establishes itself on an island, however, it is likely to find that there are very few customers for the abundant and varied supply of food, and that the choice open to it is wide. Birds in the colonising group which have larger bills than the norm for the species will thus tend to be better fed than birds with average or smaller-sized bills, if only because they have access to larger as well as smaller grades of prey. When they breed they may do so more successfully for this reason, and their offspring will inherit the tendency to have larger bills. Thus the species will get larger at least in bill length. Good examples of this in the area covered by this book are *Bebrornis* and *Terpsiphone* in Seychelles, and the drongo *Dicrurus* at Aldabra, all of which have bills disproportionately long compared with other members of their genera.

Other workers have carried the story on to include considerations of longer legs, which are also found in island as opposed to mainland birds, and allometric changes generally. There are arguments that island birds typically develop shorter wings or even become flightless, like the Aldabra Rail or the solitaire and the dodo, because over-adventurous flight is a risk on small islands, with its attendant risk of getting blown out to sea. It is true that island birds often have short wings for their size, and they also tend to have skulking habits too, compared with those of the mainland relatives. Both these characters might be related to the greater exposure of the island situation, and indeed both are permitted on the island by the relative scarcity of predators.

ISOLATION

The farther an island is from the mainland, the less chance

there is of its being reinvaded by the same species as is already established on it. Thus insular species are more or less isolated also in the sense of not having genetic material from the home population fed into their stock. As they develop their insular characteristics of large size, small clutch size, broad ecological preference, and drab coloration, these become genetically fixed in the population, which diverges from the parent stock on the continent – which may itself have evolved along a different line – until eventually the island population constitutes a new type of bird, either subspecies, species, or even genus. This geographical isolation, seen in the Galapagos Islands, was what gave Charles Darwin the idea which he later developed into his theory of Evolution. Such evolution is still not fully understood, though there have been advances since Darwin's day; studies are still going on, especially on islands, to add to the body of fact and theory.

THE BIRDS

Land and Shore Birds

NOTE. After the English, Créole, and Latin names of each species is given the plate reference and an indication of the distribution of the bird. This is shown by means of the first three letters of the name of one or more of the following places: Aldabra, Amirantes, Assumption, Astove, Cosmoledo, Farquhar, Seychelles.

Where the abbreviation is in **bold** type, breeding has been confirmed; roman type indicates that it is likely; in *italics*, the species has been recorded regularly, but not breeding; (an entry in brackets shows that the species is an occasional or rare visitor).

GREY HERON Florentin *Ardea cinerea (cinerea/firasa)* **Pl. 1**
Ald *Ass* Cos Ast Far *Ami* (Sey)

The form of this species seen in the Indian Ocean is not distinguishable in the field from the European Grey Heron. It is a tall grey-backed bird, with a noticeable black stripe along the sides of the head and black head plumes. Young birds lack the clear head markings of the adult, and have no head plumes. Legs and bill iron-grey, but may turn red or pink during breeding.

Aldabra birds at least may be hybrid between the European subspecies *cinerea* and the Malagasy *firasa*; birds from other islands in the area have not been sufficiently studied, but seem to be the same. Malagasy birds are somewhat larger than European.

The voice is a low growl.

At Aldabra the Grey Heron is conspicuous along the coastal reef flats and on the shore of the lagoon. Feeding birds are territorial, standing sentinel over a strip of shore about twenty metres long within which they will not tolerate other herons. The diet is fish including eels, which are very common in parts of Aldabra; there are records of Grey Herons chasing egrets and stealing their food. They take crabs as well, but this is not common. They are said to prey on young turtles, and they certainly take young terns, particularly Sooties, from the edges of breeding colonies in the Amirantes.

The nest is a huge untidy pile of twigs, usually built in mangroves at about head height; but on the islets in the lagoon the nest may be in very low cover or even on the ground. There are usually two eggs, pale blue in colour, though there may be as many as four. During their breeding season adults often develop pink or red legs and bill, which seems to be common in all herons; whether this is a long term change or whether it is a momentary flush is not known – but it is conspicuous in the field between March and June or July, and even into September.

Grey Herons are still hunted by man because of their predatory activities, but this does not seem to have affected their distribution; on the banks round the Amirantes they are very common and apparently on the increase. They do not breed in Seychelles, and are very rare there in the wild, but some families have one as a pet, presumably feeding it up to eat it later – it is not uncommon in the villages to see a tethered Grey Heron beside a stream.

MALAGASY SQUACCO HERON Gasse *Ardeola idae*
Ald   Pl. 1

This species is easy to identify when it is in its breeding dress, with the whole body white. The bill is black with a conspicuous blue base, and the legs are purplish-pink ('dead flesh'). In off-season dress the bird is difficult to distinguish from the European Squacco Heron, *A. ralloides*, which breeds in Madagascar alongside *A. idae*, and has been recorded in the Comoros:

the difference is that the Malagasy species is more streaky on the back. In breeding dress, however, the European bird remains brown on wings, back, and head, making it conspicuously different. The Malagasy bird is slightly larger, as if that were any help at fifty yards' range. Squaccos can be distinguished from other middle-sized herons by their characteristic squat build and hunched stance.

The voice is a rather pleasant musical 'burrrr', like the dialling tone on a telephone.

The squacco is very shy, especially when breeding; it usually feeds inland beside pools, and not often on the shore, and the most common sight of it is a single bird rising from a pool before the observer has got half close enough to see it properly. The diet consists of lizards, grasshoppers, and beetles when it is feeding inland; it probably takes crabs on the shore.

The nest is smaller than that of the Dimorphic Little Egret, and more tidily made, with small twigs laid into the fork of a bush about four to six feet off the ground. The eggs are pale blue, smaller than dimorphic, and very slightly streaked or smeared with paler blue as opposed to the clear colour of the Dimorphic Little Egret's eggs. The clutch is two or more usually three eggs, laid during November and December.

The Squacco Heron was not recorded from Aldabra before we saw it, and later found it breeding, on the Royal Society Expedition. It is not surprising that it has finally colonised Aldabra, since it migrates regularly from Madagascar to eastern Africa. The species has been recorded from Assumption, but only once, and it is not known from other islands in the area.

CATTLE EGRET Madame Paton, *Bubulcus ibis* **Pl. 1**
B.i. sechellarum: **Sey** **Ami**
B.i. ibis (indistinguishable in field): **Ald** Ass *Ast Cos Ami*

The Cattle Egret is a slim white heron, rather smaller than a Dimorphic Little Egret, from which it is distinguished by its yellow bill and all-black legs. In breeding dress the back and breast bear ginger-coloured plumes, and there is a ginger patch like a wig on the head. At the laying season the bill, face, and legs may turn pink; the eye often changes colour too. The reason for this change is not clearly known, though it is clearly connected with breeding display; one suggestion is that it is a temporary 'blush' resulting from the physiological condition of the birds, and that it comes and goes from hour to hour. If this were the case, it would help to explain the conflicting reports of different observers, some of whom say that the change does not take place at all – they might have been watching at the wrong moment. From the time when this change was first observed in the Grey Heron in Ireland (when it provoked much doubt and some ribald comment) the phenomenon has been seen in one species of heron after another, and it seems to be common to almost the whole family.

The subspecies considered here are not distinguishable in the field; this is a prime example of museum classification, in which a small difference in the colour of the breeding plumes is sufficient to separate them. This may seem niggling, but in fact it may provide a clue to the mode of dispersal of the species across the Indian Ocean.

The voice of the Cattle Egret is a harsh 'kraaaa' uttered just before the bird flies; but most of the time it is silent.

In granitic Seychelles Cattle Egrets may be seen most commonly around Victoria Market, or more typically in open grassy places, often feeding round cattle, whose movements disturb flies on which the bird feeds. They are not usually seen on the shore, save for occasional congregations round sewage outfalls or on rubbish dumps. At Aldabra they are most common by inland pools or among tortoises, which function for them in the same way as cattle. Flocks are usually small, though there is a record of sixty together at Assumption in September. Their diet is mostly insects and small land crabs – though during the breeding season of the terns on some islands they prey on eggs and chicks.

The breeding season is September–January at Aldabra, but in central Seychelles they apparently breed from April or May through to October: eggs have been found on Farquhar in August. The nests are built colonially, often in mangroves, always near or over water. The only colony so far found at Aldabra is in Bras Takamaka, where three or possibly four species of heron share a tiny islet. The nest of the Cattle Egret is a rough twiggy platform; there are three or four large blue eggs. The chicks, white from the beginning, are fed by both parents by regurgitation, apparently often with fish, which the adults do not usually eat during the rest of the year.

The first Cattle Egret was collected in Seychelles by one of the crew of H.M.S. *Rapid* in 1864; in 1878 Oustalet collected one on Cousine. They do not breed on the smaller islands now, though they are occasionally seen there. I have heard from more than one Seychellois friend an account of the introduction of the species to Seychelles near the beginning of this century; although one does not rely on such evidence as a rule, there might well be something in this story. Possibly the present Seychelles stock, which shows little if any difference from the African race, *B.i. ibis*, might be a hybrid between an old endemic race and the intro-duced birds. Early specimens of *B. ibis sechellarum* show evidence of Asiatic rather than African origin for the subspecies; perhaps it followed the same path to Seychelles as the Chinese Bittern. Cattle Egrets were deliberately introduced to Frigate and Praslin in 1960, to control flies, and they have established themselves strongly. Twelve birds were taken to Chagos from Seychelles in 1955 by one Captain Lanier, and by 1960 there were twenty-seven nests in a colony on Diego Garcia.

Cattle Egrets are predators on eggs and chicks on the seabird islands such as Bird in the central group and Desnoeufs in the Amirantes, and they raid breeding Fairy Terns on Frigate. Their expansion on that island should be watched, in case they come to be a threat to the small population of the Magpie Robin.

DIMORPHIC LITTLE EGRET   Zaigrette; Blanc et noir
Egretta garzetta dimorpha   **Pl. 1**
Ald   Cos   Ast   *Sey*

A taller and slimmer bird than the Cattle Egret, the Dimorphic
Egret is distinguished by its *black* bill with yellow facial skin, and
black legs with conspicuous *yellow* feet. Young birds may have
the yellow extending up the leg to a greater or lesser extent; the
bill of the juvenile is grey rather than black. There are two colour
phases, one white all over, the other dark slate grey with white
bastard wing coverts and chin. There are often a few mixed or
'pied' individuals in a flock, in various combinations of dark and
white. White birds seem to be more common on the seashore,
where they outnumber the dark by about three to one; in the
lagoon the ratio is less, about two to one. Elsewhere in the range
of the species the dark phase is quite uncommon. I have seen
nests which seemed to be in the charge of mixed pairs, and I have
seen pairs of mixed colours courting together, but the genetic
outcome of such pairings is not known.

The voice of the Dimorphic Egret is a harsh 'aaarrh', given
when the birds are disturbed. A breeding colony is largely
silent, but when an intruder appears the birds sound like a riot
in a rural market-place.

Dimorphic Egrets are rare inland by pools, and uncommon on
sandy shores, but on other types of shore they are common at
Aldabra, Cosmoledo, and Astove. They bred on Assumption at
least until 1906, but do so no longer. They have been recorded
from time to time in the Amirantes, and they are seen very
occasionally in Seychelles, where they appear after rough
weather. They feed in groups, not strongly territorial like the
Grey Heron, but showing irritation when another bird comes
within about a yard. They stalk their prey, sometimes using
curious little flapping movements of the foot, perhaps to drive
a small fish out of cover. When the prey is sighted, the egret often
chases it wildly in the shallows, all pretence of stalking gone, in a
flurry of legs and wings. In shallow water over a bare substrate
they are to be seen flying up a little way and plunging down on

fish, a variation of the wing-shading technique seen in other herons, to improve their view of the prey. The diet is small fish and eels, sometimes crabs, and occasionally, during the breeding season, insects.

The Dimorphic Egret breeds from November to February at Aldabra, usually in colonies. The nest is a rough platform, larger than that of a Cattle Egret or Squacco Heron, built in cover between three and seven feet high. The clutch is two or three large pale blue eggs, and the chicks are greyish white when they hatch; but as soon as the first feathers of the juvenile plumage begin to sprout, the colour phase of the chick can be determined. Both parents feed the chicks, by regurgitation; the chicks leave the nest relatively early, but they are fed by the parents for several weeks thereafter.

Although the Dimorphic Egret is not a tame species, it seems little disturbed by human activity on the shore, and may be approached quite closely by someone walking in the water. At the nest it is quite confiding, returning quickly after being accidentally put off: this is probably necessary, since in the denser colonies chicks are often attacked by the adult occupants of neighbouring nests.

The nominate subspecies *E. g. garzetta* occurs all round the coast of the African mainland; *dimorpha* is the subspecies both on Madagascar and in the Aldabras, though some workers have suggested that the birds of Aldabra and Assumption should be separated on account of being rather larger. They are distinct as a breeding group, but they are not now regarded as a separate subspecies.

GREEN-BACKED HERON Mannique *Butorides striatus*
B. s. degens: **Sey**   **Pl. 1**
B. s. crawfordi: **Ald Ass Ami** *Cos Ast* Far

The two subspecies of the Green-backed Heron which occur on the islands covered by this book are barely distinguishable in the field, but of course they are never seen together. They are both small hunch-backed herons, brown and more or less streaky on the back, greyish and more evenly coloured below. Juveniles are less evenly marked than adults, and heavily streaked below. Green-backed Herons are very shy, often to be seen flying away from the observer rather fast, with a characteristic call, a short nasal 'aahnk'.

The species may be seen feeding on the shore, of the sea and of the lagoon, often in mangroves, and also quite often inland, especially at Aldabra. It feeds by waiting motionless for its prey, truly heronlike, not actively hunting like a Dimorphic Egret. Its diet is fish and crabs, also insects and lizards at Aldabra; but it is seldom seen away from the shore in Seychelles, probably because of the potential competition with other birds such as mynahs and the more numerous Cattle Egrets.

The nest of the Green-backed Heron is usually built away from others, though there is some evidence of colonial building at Aldabra. If this is confirmed, Aldabra is the only place where the species is colonial. The structure is small, about a foot across, made of thin twigs in a shallow bowl shape. The normal clutch is two to three slightly mottled pale blue eggs. At Aldabra the breeding season seems to extend from November to January, but in Seychelles there have been nesting records from all months of the year. However, the species is rare in Seychelles, and the data are rather thin, so that this should be checked.

There have been one or two records of changes in leg and bill colour at Aldabra, to pale pink or bright red from the normal horn colour, but this has never been seen in Seychelles.

Compared with the abundance of *crawfordi* in the Amirantes and at Aldabra, *degens* is rare in Seychelles. This is probably because nesting sites are becoming scarce as more of the mangroves are cut out: in places where mangroves persist, as at L'Amitié on Praslin, or Port Glaud, Mahé, the bird is relatively easy to see; elsewhere it is at best an occasional visitor.

The relations of the Green-backed Heron are numerous and widespread, and in one respect at least of great interest. The subspecies in the Comoros, *B. s. rhizophorae*, in the Mascarenes, *B. s. javanicus*, and on Aldabra, are all considered to be of Asian origin. The subspecies of the African mainland, *B. s. atricapillus*, has apparently given rise to *B. s. rutenbergi* of Madagascar, but also, surprisingly, to *degens*, the subspecies in Seychelles. This, at any rate, is the opinion of White (1951) after his study of the species. The reason for this overlap in distribution is not known, though perhaps modern serological methods might reveal some degree of hybridisation which would help to explain it.

CHINESE BITTERN *Ixobrychus sinensis* Pl. 1
Sey

A small heron-like bird, the colour of dead reeds, a mixture of streaky yellows and browns, with yellow bill and legs, the Chinese Bittern is a very difficult bird to see. It is shy in its behaviour as well as cryptic in colour, and it has the habit common to all bitterns of 'freezing' when alarmed, adopting a rigid pose with the bill pointing upwards, which makes it almost invisible among the reeds. It is mostly crepuscular (dusk-active) or nocturnal in its movements, too, presenting all in all something of a challenge to the bird-watcher.

It is to be seen in the swamps behind L'Amitié, Praslin, and probably also in swamps in the remoter parts of La Digue and Mahé, but it is rare. Its habitat is restricted by its preference for fresh water. Its diet is unknown, but would include frogs and lizards, and also such brackish-water fish as mud-skippers and gudgeon.

The nest site is given by Lalanne (1963) as 'high up on trees near marshes and rivers'. For a bittern the site described is most unusual. Other species nest much nearer the ground; among reeds, usually at water level, in a marsh or near the edge of a river. Lalanne gives the clutch as 'two pale blue eggs', and the breeding season as continuous throughout the year, but much more information is needed on this and other points of the biology of this very secretive species.

Little indeed is known of the Chinese Bittern in Seychelles. Vesey-FitzGerald, who wrote in 1936 the first modern account of the bird life of the islands, was of the opinion that it is a naturally occurring species, and I agree. For one thing, it is difficult to imagine anyone introducing such an inconspicuous bird. It has been objected that the bittern does not occur in the island groups on either side of Seychelles, but these places do not have substantial areas of fresh water, indeed some of the islands have no surface fresh water at all. Since bitterns are fresh water birds, it is quite likely that they could only establish themselves in the high islands, where fresh or at least brackish water is relatively abundant. Hence the discontinuous distribution in the islands, and hence also the distance from the edge of the normal range of the species; there is nowhere else in between where it could occur. If it is a natural colonist, it is quite probably a very recent arrival: Seychelles birds are indistinguishable from those of Asia, the home of the species.

ALDABRA SACRED IBIS Ribis *Threskiornis aethiopica abbotti*   **Pl. 2**
Ald

The Sacred Ibis is unmistakable, large and white, with the head and neck bald and black. A large 'bustle' of blue-black plumes (sometimes brownish, in younger birds) is a conspicuous feature. The legs are black. However, the observer should look closely at the wingtips and eye of isolated birds: in the Aldabra subspecies the eye is china-blue in adults, and the wings have very short black tips or none at all. In the nominate African subspecies, which has been recorded once from Aldabra, the eye is brownish-red, and the wings have noticeable black tips, about fifty millimetres long. Such birds can only be rare vagrants from the African population. The voice of the Aldabra Sacred Ibis is a weary groan, more squeaky when alarmed. During the breeding season the adults have a patch of bright red skin under the 'armpits', which usually fades to dull purple or brown out of season. Juveniles have the head and neck feathered, greyish white with a few black spots, and brown eyes.

The ibis is rare on Picard (West) Island, because it has been so harassed by man, and it is very uncommon on Polymnie and Middle Islands, for reasons which are not clear. On South Island, particularly at the eastern end, it is fairly common along the lagoon shore, and more so around pools among the *platin* inland, where small groups may be seen feeding. Even so, there may not be more than 150 individual birds on Aldabra. The diet is most commonly crabs, either dug out of the muddy lagoon shore or caught by pools, but snails and large insects are also eaten, and the ibis is a constant scavenger round human camps and dead tortoises and turtles. Ibises were at one time extremely tame at Aldabra, and though the adults are more wary now, after a century or more of contact with man the ibis-eater, the juveniles are still extremely trusting and very curious.

Ibises nest in November–December, in dense colonies in low bushes near or over pools, the nests ramshackle piles of twigs arranged in a rough cup, lined with leaves and grass, and often decorated with green leafy branches. The clutch is usually two large white eggs, rarely one or three. Breeding colonies are *very susceptible to disturbance*, and are usually abandoned after a visit by man. If one is located, it should not be approached at all, even if the birds do not seem disturbed at the time – see Benson and Penny (1971) for proof of this. The birds at a breeding colony, or on a crowded roosting tree, fight often amongst themselves, fencing with their bills, or jumping and kicking at each other like gamecocks. When feeding, however, they seem tolerant of each other's presence.

The status of the ibis at Aldabra might be less secure than it seems, for although the species is no longer hunted, under the protection of the Government, its sensitivity on the breeding colony makes it very vulnerable to even occasional disturbance at just the wrong time of year.

There are three subspecies of *Threskiornis aethiopica*, the nominate *aethiopica*, which is widespread over Africa, the Malagasy *bernieri*, with small black wingtips and a white eye, which has not so far been seen at Aldabra but might occur there, and *abbotti*, which occurs only at Aldabra and never seems to have been seen anywhere else.

GREATER FLAMINGO Flamant *Phoenicopterus ruber roseus*
Ald (Sey)   **Pl. 2**

A spectacular sight, and unmistakable, the Greater Flamingo is
one of the many puzzles of Aldabra. It has been seen since the
middle of the last century, when Abbott mentioned between 500
and 1,000 of the species, but numbers are variable in these
records. The place is nearly always the same, at the eastern end of
the atoll; during the Royal Society Expedition in 1967, we saw
a maximum of fifty-five birds, always in the same limited area:
either at Bassin Flamant, the most regular place for the birds, or
in the flooded area behind Bras Cinq Cases at spring tides, or
behind Ile aux Cèdres, in an almost inaccessible part of the
lagoon.

Flamingos feed by sieving water through a complicated
system of filters in the bill, using the tongue as a pump. Their
diet at Aldabra is not known, but presumably it consists of small
invertebrates and plant material as it does in Africa.

The status of the flock at Aldabra is a mystery. It may be an
assembly of vagrants which have drifted over from Africa during
the migratory season at odd times, who are now living out their
days in this dead end; or perhaps it is a regular migrant flock.
There have been very few records between May and August,
which tends to support the latter idea, but on the other hand
there have been very few observers at Aldabra at that time of
year. If it is merely a group of vagrants, it is hard to understand
why the species has not been reported from time to time from,
say, the lagoon at Cosmoledo. Marking experiments to find how
long individual birds are likely to stay on the atoll would be of
enormous interest; just how they would be done, I leave to
someone else. It is the occurrence of birds like this which makes
Aldabra such an exciting place.

A recent record (Beamish, 1972, pers. comm.) reports two
Greater Flamingos on the 'reclaim' in Victoria Harbour,
where they excited great curiosity among the local inhabitants.
They remained from December, 1971, to March, 1972, by
which time they had completed a moult.

MADAGASCAR KESTREL Katiti *Falco newtoni* **Pl. 3**
Ald

A small brightly coloured kestrel, creamy and streaked below, and chestnut with a few black markings on the wings and mantle, the Aldabra Katiti is a fairly conspicuous bird. It perches habitually on bare poles (there is often one on the flagpole at the Settlement), and it may be seen hovering against the wind over dunes on the south coast. It is very tame and approachable when perched. Its voice gives it its name – a thin chattering 'tititi'.

The sightings of kestrels at Aldabra seem nearly always to have been in the same places; around the Settlement, at Anse Mais, and towards the eastern end of South Island. There are only very few records from Polymnie or Middle Island. The diet at Aldabra includes lizards, rats, and large insects.

The only nest ever seen on Aldabra was in a coconut palm at Anse Mais, in the bowl-shaped base of a frond. It contained three young birds, still downy in December, suggesting that the eggs were laid during November. The Bristol Seychelles Expedition found the nest by watching the comings and goings of a pair of adults which were carrying food, mostly lizards. Both parents were actively defending the nest against the attentions of two Pied Crows, driving them away with fierce attacks. Coconut palms are not common at Aldabra except round the Settlement and at Anse Mais; at the eastern end of the atoll the birds must nest somewhere else, perhaps in the dead crown of a *Pandanus* palm, or in the fork of a large tree.

It has been suggested that the kestrel is a very recent colonist of Aldabra, perhaps since man arrived there. Certainly it is not now regarded as distinct from the Madagascar species, although it is somewhat smaller; and it is probably the least numerous of the birds of Aldabra, not apparently through any persecution or predation, which suggests again that it may only just be establishing itself on the atoll.

The Madagascar Kestrel is related to *Falco tinnunculus* of southern Africa; and in some way it must have given rise to the

Seychelles Kestrel, *F. araea*. The other kestrel of the region, *F. punctatus* of Mauritius, is also related in some way, but quite how the three are linked is not clear. One would suggest that Mauritius and Seychelles were colonised separately from Madagascar, but there is no evidence to build on at all.

SEYCHELLES KESTREL   Katiti   *Falco araea*   Pl. 3
Sey

The Seychelles Kestrel is much smaller than the Aldabra species, and it lacks the mottling below; its upper parts are more heavily marked with black. It is unmistakable in Seychelles because of its very small size; any of the occasional vagrant hawks in the islands are much larger.

A kestrel may be seen almost anywhere on Mahé or Silhouette, though rarely on Praslin or La Digue. Each bird has one or more favourite perches, which it uses day after day; these are prominent look-out points, such as the bare branch of a tree, an electricity pole, or the ridge of a house. From here the bird surveys the ground, occasionally darting down on a lizard or a large insect; and from here it starts the lazy sweeping searches which carry it over its extensive territory in search of prey. As on Aldabra, the voice of the kestrel gives it its name, a thin mewing 'titititi'. The diet in Seychelles consists of lizards and large insects, and occasionally small birds such as white-eyes. The alternative Créole name for the bird is 'manzeur des poules' – chicken eater – but this is undeserved, for at most this tiny hawk could take a few chicks.

The nest of the kestrel must at one time have been in rocks on the mountainside, but these sites are now largely occupied by introduced Barn Owls, as are the church towers which used to be a common site for kestrel nests; now kestrels nest mainly in the open roofs of houses, where a few sticks support the clutch of one or two white eggs, liberally marked with brown. Both parents carry food to the young, and at least one parent is to be seen on guard near the nest during the fledging period. The breeding season is from September or October to March.

Undoubtedly the kestrel was once much more common in Seychelles than it is now. The destruction of its forest habitat, and the planting of the relatively barren coconut plantation which has replaced it in the lowlands, coupled with the introduction of rats and cats – and Barn Owls – have all tended to make life more difficult for the bird. The territories which exist now are very large, and although the kestrel is quite a common sight, it may not be very numerous in Seychelles. Each pair has to have such a large area in which to hunt now that prey is so scarce, that there is simply not room for any more birds. This scarcity makes it all the more unfortunate that some Seychellois still regard the bird as unlucky, an omen of death, and kill it if it approaches their house too closely. There may not be more than 200 kestrels on Mahé, partly because of the silly superstition which leads to so many being killed in what is now their favourite breeding site. In fact, a pair of kestrels in the roof is a source of pleasure to many enlightened people in the islands, and one might hope that this attitude will spread.

The relatives of the kestrel are discussed in the section on the Aldabra bird.

GREY FRANCOLIN   Perdrix(?)   *Francolinus pondicerianus*
Ami   (Sey in captivity)   **Pl. 2**

Grey Francolins were introduced on to some islands as sporting birds, and at one time evidently they were quite widespread: however, they failed to survive except on Desroches, where they are now feral. On some estates in Seychelles they are reared in captivity for the table, as is the Chinese Francolin, *F. pintadeanus*.

The Grey Francolin is hard to confuse with any other bird on Desroches: it is nearly the size of a chicken, barred dark brown and cream above, and black below; the head is rather smartly patterned, with yellow cheeks and a white throat. The legs are dark red, with pronounced spurs in the male. The call of the francolin is a rather high-pitched chicken-like 'claaaak'.

Francolins nest on the ground, usually in thick cover, laying up

Plate 1   HERONS, EGRETS AND BITTERNS

1. **Malagasy Squacco Heron**   *Ardeola idae*   p. 50
Squat build. All white in breeding dress, streaky brown
non-breeding. Bill black, blue at base.

2. **Dimorphic Little Egret**   *Egretta garzetta dimorpha*   p. 54
Taller than Cattle Egret, from which white phase may also
be distinguished by yellow feet and longer black bill. Adults
have long head plumes. Mixed-phase birds not uncommon.
a, Dark phase.
b, White phase.

3. **Grey Heron**   *Ardea cinerea*   p. 49
Broad black stripe on otherwise whitish head. Very tall;
solitary in shallow water.

4. **Cattle Egret**   *Bubulcus ibis*   p. 51
White with yellow bill and dark legs (both liable to turn
reddish when breeding). Ginger plumes in breeding dress,
as illustrated.

5. **Green-backed Heron**   *Butorides striatus*   p. 55
Hunched, streaky bird of the shore; solitary in shallow water.
a, *B.s. degens* Central Seychelles, possible Amirantes.
b, *B.s. crawfordi* Elsewhere in the area. Only slightly more
colourful than Seychelles bird, but the two subspecies not
likely to occur together.

6. **Chinese Bittern**   *Ixobrychus sinensis*   p. 57
Yellowish, streaky, retiring bird, occasionally seen in reedy
swamps. Short legs, thick-looking neck, habit of 'freezing'
when disturbed, all characteristic.

IBIS, FLAMINGO, FRANCOLIN, MOORHEN AND RAIL

Plate 2

1. Grey Francolin *Francolinus pondicerianus*   p. 63
Chicken-sized game bird; streaky appearance and rapid movement distinguish from domestic fowl. Feral, Desroches only.

2. Greater Flamingo *Phoenicopterus ruber roseus*   p. 60
Difficult to mistake for any other bird. Regular eastern end of Aldabra only, but two seen Victoria Harour 1971.

3. Aldabra Sacred Ibis *Threskiornis aethiopica abbotti*   p. 58
Unmistakeable. Pools and occasionally shoreline at Aldabra.
a, Adult: white with black plumes and bald head and neck, china-blue eyes.
b, Juvenile: brown plumes, feathered head and neck gradually becoming bald during first year; eyes brown when young, gradually changing to blue, via white.

4. Flightless White-throated Rail *Dryolimnas cuvieri*   p. 67
aldabranus
Small olive-green bird seen Middle Island and Polymnie, Aldabra. Juveniles dark brown, eyes altering from olive-green to adult chestnut.
a, Female: brighter red base to bill, smaller.
b, Male: dusty red base to bill, larger.

5. Moorhen (*Common Gallinule*)   *Gallinula chloropus*   p. 66
meridionalis
Black with red frontal shield in adults; conspicuous black and white undertail seen in retreat. Juveniles brown; lack frontal shield.

to ten eggs in a rather casual-looking nest of twigs and grasses. The young are nidifugous, following the mother, who shows them feeding places, and turns the ground for them in the early stages, but does not actually feed them. They eat mostly insects, though they will take seeds like the adults, when they are available.

Being a dry country bird, the francolin is well adapted to survive on coral islands once it has been introduced – provided that it is not shot out. It seems to have no adverse effect on the rest of the community on Desroches, being more in the nature of a historical curiosity than a true coloniser.

In November, 1971, there were two Grey Francolins on African Island, far to the north of Desroches, but a fortnight later they were gone.

MOORHEN (COMMON GALLINULE)   Poule d'eau
Gallinula chloropus meridionalis   **Pl. 2**
Sey

The Seychelles Moorhen looks just like its European or African counterpart: it is black, laterally compressed (like a flea and for much the same reason), and it has a red frontal shield, white under tail feathers, and very long toes. Its voice is a series of chicken-like clucks, with a piercing squawk when it is alarmed. Although it is quite common in marshy places away from habitation, it is hard to see because it is so shy. Watching moorhens in Seychelles is a test of one's endurance of mosquitoes; it might be called a bird-watcher's bird. The diet is catholic: snails and small lizards are the basic ingredients, with insects and such plant material as reed shoots, and crops such as sweet potatoes and even bananas.

The nest is built near water, sometimes actually among the reeds themselves, often above water level on the bank; one on Cousin was eight feet up on a rock beside a pool. The nest is a deep cup of coarse grass and coconut fibres, up to a foot across, and it may contain anything from four to ten eggs, beige in ground colour with light speckling in purple and brown. The first and last chicks hatch within two or three days of each other; they are nidifugous, like all gallinules, being able to run and swim almost from birth. They are led rather than fed by the parents. A young bird, perhaps from a previous clutch, helped two adults to rear a brood of eight on Cousin. The downy chicks are black above and greyish below, with a patch of red skin on the head which is lost in the first juvenile plumage.

The past distribution of moorhens in Seychelles is not known, but presumably they were more common when there was more undrained swampy land. They are still not rare to-day, though they are not often seen. Although they are not strong fliers, moorhens are quite common on remote islands all over the world, and there is no evidence that they were introduced by man in Seychelles. They have been the object of human predation, though now they are protected by law. However, the traps which can still be found in some villages look in rather good repair. The birds are pretty effectively protected, by their shyness and mobility through the dense reeds, against attacks by man; they have also survived predation by rats, probably because their nests are surrounded by a natural moat.

While watching moorhens, keep an eye open for the Black Marsh Terrapin, which lives in the same sort of place and is just about as shy.

FLIGHTLESS WHITE-THROATED RAIL   Chiumicho
Dryolimnas cuvieri aldabranus   **Pl. 2**
Ald   (??**Cos**)

The Flightless Rail is probably the most famous bird of Aldabra. It is a small olive-green rail, with a chestnut head and a conspicuous white throat-patch; the bill is dark horn colour, with a red patch at the base of the upper mandible. In females this patch is bright pink, and in males rather dark dusty red. The bird has short wings, with a modified feather structure which makes them quite unsuited for flight; when it runs it does so very fast with its wings extended backwards. It uses the wings only in scaling rocks or tree stumps, when it shows the flying abilities of the average domestic hen. The voice is a wide range of grunts and squeals, but the most conspicuous sound is the mating call, a series of high-pitched squeals delivered by two birds as a duet. This is heard commonly from September through to March, especially in the morning and evening or after a shower of rain.

The rail is now found on Polymnie and Middle Islands, Michel, and Ile aux Cèdres, as well as on the innumerable islets along the south side of Middle Island. It is extinct on Settlement Island and South Island. It is most easily seen in the open scrub along the north side of Middle Island, running in and out of the bush. The legendary way to attract rails is by tapping turtle bones together – and it works; however, any disturbance is sufficient to bring rails to the spot in search of food. Probably the best way is to walk about a little, and then sit down; within a few minutes there will be a rail on the spot to see what's up, and their tameness is such that it will probably peck at your clothing if you sit still! Rails are omnivorous, though they seem to take insects more often than other foods. The habit of investigating any noise seems to derive from their way of feeding among the leaf litter disturbed by passing tortoises, like Cattle Egrets following ungulates.

The breeding season of the rail at Aldabra is October through to February or March: the nest is a deep cup of *Casuarina* and grass, built in the low fork of a bush, very well concealed. The clutch is three or four eggs, white with reddish speckling. The chicks are shiny black when they hatch, with olive-green eyes; as they grow up and acquire the adult plumage, the eye changes to the adult colour of orange. The parents are very aggressive in defence of nest and chicks, displaying and charging at the observer without fear.

The rail was found all over Aldabra until cats became common on South and Settlement Islands and wiped it out. It is evidently able to live with rats, which are common on Middle Island at least; and it has survived in the past quite heavy human predation on Aldabra. It is now protected there by law, but it is too late to protect the species on Assumption and Astove, and on most if not all of Cosmoledo, where a combination of cats and men have caused its extinction. It is just possible that rails might survive on South Island, Cosmoledo, which has not been visited since 1906, when there were rails there. In its present range, failing the development of the airbase on Aldabra, the rail is fairly safe, provided that there is no further spread of cats.

The relatives of the Aldabra Rail are the nominate *Dryolimnas cuvieri cuvieri* of Madagascar (extinct on Mauritius – man again), and the form extinct from Assumption and the other islands, thought to have been a distinct subspecies, *D. c. abotti*.

The Aldabra Rail is the last surviving flightless bird of the Indian Ocean, albeit a member of a genus which is renowned for going flightless on islands. It is not as odd as the Dodo or the Solitaire of Mauritius or Réunion, but nevertheless it is in some sense a memorial to them, and as such it should be preserved by any means at our disposal.

COMORO BLUE PIGEON   Pigeon hollandais
Alectroenas sganzini minor   **Pl. 3**
Ald

Named after the Dutch flag, which at the time of the first exploration of the Indian Ocean islands was the only tricolour – the first of many – this is a striking silvery white pigeon with blue wings and tail and a ravishing 'Egyptian eye' surrounded by red skin. Plume feathers round the neck of adults are silver with a tiny red tip, which shows up in display as a faint pink halo round the head when the ruff is raised. The voice is a hoarse deep 'hough hough' repeated four or five times.

Blue Pigeons are not common at the western end of Aldabra, but in the east, particularly round East Channel and Cinq Cases, they may be seen twenty at a time in fruiting trees. Perched on a bare branch in the heat of the day, they are extremely tame and approachable, which has led to their reduction or extinction on several islands; but the limit to their distribution on Aldabra is more probably set by the distribution of suitable feeding trees

than by the occasional human predation; the western end seems
never to have had many of this species. The diet is fleshy fruits
of all kinds, including the 'marbles' of Takamaka trees, and *Ficus*
species.

The nest is a typical pigeon platform, roughly made in the
fork of a mangrove or another tree, and usually well concealed;
the clutch is one white egg, laid in December as a rule. From
September onwards the display flight is commonly seen, rather
like that of the Wood Pigeon, *Columba palumbus*: the bird climbs
steeply in the air, and then glides down in a rigid pose with the
wings held forward and down.

Blue Pigeons are not recorded from other islands in the
Aldabra group; there is a record dated 1821 of one (species
unknown) which was common in Providence and Farquhar, but
is now extinct. Otherwise this Indian Ocean genus has four other
representatives: nominate *A. s. sganzini* from Comoros, said to be
declining under human predation; *A. madagascariensis* in
Madagascar; *A. nitidissima* from Mauritius, extinct a century or
more; and *A. pulcherrima* in Seychelles.

Because they are so good to eat, Blue Pigeons as a group have
declined sharply since men first came to the islands, but with
their present total protection at Aldabra, and with their capture
illegal in Seychelles, they might hopefully survive from now on.

SEYCHELLES BLUE PIGEON   Pigeon hollandais
Alectroenas pulcherrima   **Pl. 3**
Sey

This is a spectacular creature, similar to *A. sganzini* of Aldabra,
but with a shiny convoluted wattle on the head, like a scarlet
walnut. The white and blue are distributed as in the Aldabra
species, and the Seychelles bird also has the crimson tip to the
neck plumes, which it uses in display in the same way. The blue
of wings and tail has a red sheen in strong sunlight, which the
Aldabra bird seems to lack. There is no sexual difference in
plumage, but the breeding male has a larger and more convoluted wattle. The voice is a deep hoarse cooing.

The Blue Pigeon is to be seen wherever the mountain forest persists, most commonly on Praslin, but also in remote parts of Mahé, on Silhouette, and on Frigate. The diet is fruits, including Takamaka 'marbles', which are crammed into the crop in dozens, wild guavas, and cinnamon berries. The birds feed voraciously in groups in fruiting trees, and then sit motionless for hours in the shade afterwards, quite inconspicuous in their disruptive colours.

The nest is the usual 'pigeon platform', as at Aldabra, but the clutch may be one or two, instead of always one. The female builds alone, not helped by the male, but both sexes share the job of incubation and rearing the chicks. The young are highly cryptic in colouring, greenish-grey mottled with pale yellow. The same display flight is seen, very impressive when the birds swoop down over the palms of the Vallée de Mai.

The Blue Pigeon was much more common in the past, when landowners treated the large flocks round their fruit groves as useful edible assets. Partly as a result of over-cropping, and partly because fruit groves no longer form a large part of agriculture in Seychelles, the bird is less common now. The Barn Owl probably takes a number of Blue Pigeons, especially young birds, and some are still taken illegally with bird lime, though the authorities are trying to stop this senseless predation.

One aspect of the physiology of this particular group of pigeons (the subfamily Treroninae) affects their conservation: members of this subfamily have muscular gizzards which are capable of breaking up and digesting seeds. This means that their droppings, unlike those of other pigeons, do not contain viable seeds, so that fruit pigeons do not spread their food plants as other pigeons do. They therefore depend much more for survival on the conservation of their habitat, and suffer correspondingly more from its destruction.

TURTLE DOVE Tourterelle (des Iles) *Streptopelia picturata*
Ald Ami Sey   **Pl. 3**

There are four subspecies of this species in the islands covered by this book; they all look at least superficially similar, and they share the same mode of life, so I shall take them all together. They are distinguished by locality more than by their appearance, though there are small differences of size and colour between the island races. They are stout grey-brown birds, with a more or less reddish head and mantle, and purple feet and legs, which turn red in the breeding season. The voice is very dove-like, a low burbling 'crr-rrooo'.

The only two subspecies which may have to be distinguished in the field are *Streptopelia p. picturata*, the Malagasy form, and *S. p. rostrata*, the endemic form of Seychelles, which occur together in Seychelles, the former having been introduced. On all except one or two small islands (Cousin, Cousine, and perhaps Frigate), *picturata* has displaced or diluted *rostrata*. On the islands where the characters of the endemic race survive, the differences between the two races are these: *rostrata* has a vinous red head, a chestnut mantle, and grey-brown under tail feathers, and is much smaller; and *picturata* has a grey head, purplish mantle, white under the tail, and is larger. Many birds must be hybrid, but on Mahé and Praslin the predominant appearance is *picturata*-like. Measurements of wing-lengths would be of great interest from these islands: some which I took on Cousin indicated that the average is halfway between 170 millimetres, the average length of pure *picturata*, and around 150 millimetres, the wing length of the few pure specimens of *rostrata* in museums. This suggests that even on Cousin, where there are not a few of the endemic type to be seen, there has been a considerable degree of interbreeding. The names and distribution of the other subspecies are given in the last paragraph of this account; first I shall describe their biology as a group.

The distribution of Turtle Doves on all the islands where they live is decided by their food supply, though their scarcity in western Aldabra may point to some human predation. They are principally seed and fruit eaters, feeding mostly on the ground and in the shade. On Aldabra they congregate under *Casuarina* trees; in Seychelles the seeds of the Castor plant, *Ricinus*, are very popular. Since this plant is often grown near houses, however, dangerous places for edible birds at least in the recent past, its seeds are not much taken on Mahé and Praslin. On these islands the birds are most common up on the mountain roads, where they feed on the seeds of the roadside plants. On the smaller islands, such as Cousin and Frigate, where protection can be more rigorously enforced, the doves are seen round the houses, and also on copra driers, where they feed on drying coconut meat.

The nest is a platform, often in *Casuarina*, or in mangroves at Aldabra; the clutch is two white eggs in Seychelles and Aldabra. The young are fed on 'pigeon milk', a cheesy substance consisting of the regurgitated cellular lining of the crop of the adult. This is very similar in its fat and protein content to mammalian milk; to ensure its purity, the adults fast for several hours before feeding the young. Pigeons are among the few types of bird which do not feed their young with animals during the first few days of life – evidently the milk is a satisfactory substitute.

At the start of the breeding season, around October, Turtle Doves may be seen fighting at the borders of their territories, circling each other and delivering mighty blows with their wings. These combats go on day after day in the same place, until the border is established by the stronger bird.

The past distribution of the subspecies was as follows: *S. p. picturata* on Madagascar; *S. p. rostrata* in central Seychelles; *S. p. aldabrana* (a misnomer) in the Amirantes; *S. p. coppingeri* at Aldabra and Assumption, and probably also Cosmoledo and Astove; and *S. p. comorensis* in the Comoros. This situation has broken down now, largely because of the introduction of *picturata* into Seychelles, probably by the release of some birds which were being carried as a food supply on one of the early ships. Now the Seychelles stock is nearly all hybrid, as I have suggested above. *Aldabrana* still survives in small numbers in the Amirantes, where, however, it has been mixed with *picturata* introduced from Seychelles; and on Aldabra itself *coppingeri* is common, though it is extinct on Assumption and Cosmoledo, assuming that it was this subspecies which once occurred on those islands. The subspecies in the Chagos islands, by the way, has been shown to be hybrid, *picturata* × *comorensis*, and it probably arrived in the same way as the Seychelles immigrants, as excess food stores on a pirate ship.

The genus *Streptopelia* is widely represented all over Africa and southern Europe.

BARRED GROUND DOVE　Tourterelle coco
Geopelia striata　　　　　　　　　　　　　　　　**Pl. 3**
Cos　Far　Sey

A small buff-coloured dove, barred with black above and on the neck and breast, the underparts more reddish. Round the eye and at the base of the bill the exposed skin is a clear pale blue. The tail is long and narrow, as in all *Geopelia*, but when it is spread in the courtship display the white outer feathers emphasise its triangular shape. The voice is a rhythmic staccato cooing, much higher pitched than that of the turtle doves.

The Barred Ground Dove is one of the three most common land birds in Seychelles, to be seen all over the islands, especially round houses. It is common on Farquhar, but rather scarce at present on Cosmoledo. It is readily tamed; although it is basically a seed-eater it has adapted its diet to commensalism with man, like the other successful introduced species, the mynah and the cardinal. Away from habitation it is most commonly seen among the undergrowth of lowland plantations; it is rather rare in the hills.

The breeding season is almost continuous, but there is a noticeable peak in activity during the north-west monsoon from November to March, coinciding with the hot weather and an increase in the amount of seeds available. The elegant courtship of the males, bowing and flicking out their tail feathers, is especially conspicuous at this time. Despite its habit of feeding on the ground, the Ground Dove often nests high up, building a nest which is unusually compact for a dove, with grass blades and *Casuarina* leaves laid on a platform of coarser material, often as much as thirty feet from the ground. On islands such as

Cousin, where there are no rats, Ground Dove nests may be found lower down, usually among clumps of bracken. The clutch is two white eggs; both parents share in incubation and in the rearing of the young, which hatch helpless, covered in dirty yellowish down. The squabs can fly after only three weeks, when they look very similar to their parents, but paler in colour and with very short tails.

At night and in cold wet weather, Ground Doves roost in trees, hunched and fluffed out, looking alternately like kestrels, Scops Owls, and other rare birds.

They were introduced into Seychelles from India via Mauritius, the same route as the mynah, probably by Indian traders; in 1960 they were introduced into Chagos by a Seychellois called Raymond Mein.

MADAGASCAR COUCAL Toulou *Centropus toulou insularis*
Ald (?Ass)   **Pl. 6**

Unmistakable; a large rather shy black bird with a long glossy black tail and chestnut wings in breeding dress, the black replaced by streaky brown in the off-season. The bill is black in breeding and brown out of season. The voice is a musical and rather eerie laugh, descending almost a full octave ('hoo-hoo-hoo . . .'). Pairs often duet, or answer one another over long distances.

The coucal usually skulks in dense bush, occasionally in deep mangroves, except in the morning and evening, when it may perch high at the top of a tree to sing. It moves easily on foot, both in cover and on open ground. Despite its size and its striking colour in the breeding season, it is inconspicuous; often the first sign of one is the call, either the 'laugh' or a chattering alarm sound, given from deep cover close behind a passer-by. It feeds on large insects, lizards, and quite probably also the eggs and young of smaller birds, judging from the way in which it is mobbed by sunbirds and cardinals, which treat it as a public enemy.

The nest is a large barrel-shaped horizontal tube with the entrance at one end, low in a bush. The breeding season seems to be during the north-west monsoon, from November to March. The clutch recorded by W. L. Abbott in 1893 was of three or four eggs in December; M. J. Nicoll found a nest with two young on Assumption in mid-March. No other details of the breeding of this species are known.

The subspecies *assumptionis*, named from Assumption, is not regarded as distinct from *insularis* of Aldabra; coucals have not definitely been seen on Assumption since 1937, and are probably extinct there by now. They have never been recorded from anywhere else in the group. At Aldabra coucals are fairly common on West Island, but they are much more common in the east of the atoll, along with the many other species which have suffered at least to some extent from human disturbance.

Apart from the dubious *assumptionis*, there is one other sub-species, nominate *toulou*, from Madagascar, very similar to *insularis*. The relations within the genus are not at all clear: apparently *C. toulou* is not much like *C. grillii* of Africa or *C. bengalensis* of Asia, but might be more closely related to *C. sinensis*, from even farther east.

BLACK PARROT   Cateau noir,   *Coracopsis nigra barklyi*
Sey   **Pl. 4**

Dark grey-brown, not black, with a grey bill and black legs, the Black Parrot can hardly be mistaken for anything else when it is perched; but on the wing it can often look like a Blue Pigeon, in silhouette against a bright sky. It has less pointed wings, however, and a bullet-headed appearance, and it flies more quickly and directly. Its voice is a series of high-pitched whistles, clear and urchin-like, sometimes broken into a series of staccato notes. To add to the complication, many of the mynahs on Praslin imitate it very accurately.

The parrot is seen only on Praslin, most often round the remark-able reserve in the Vallée de Mai. It is very shy of man; to see it you will need to be quiet in your movements, and preferably not in a large group of people. Once it is in view it is a charming sight, climbing acrobatically among the branches with beak and claws, or swinging upside down on the male flowers of the Coco de Mer. Its diet is fruit and flowers, including the introduced Chinese Guava and the buds of Bois Rouge. Often birds can be seen sunning themselves with drooping wings in a quiet corner, but the most common sighting is of a dark bird sailing high over the trees.

The courtship is a graceful business, the partners bowing and tucking to each other and touching bills. Rather little is known of the breeding behaviour. The season seems to extend through the north-west monsoon, for although nests have been found in November, other pairs are still courting in February. Only two nests have ever been seen, both by Philippe Lalanne; one contained three young birds, and the other two white eggs. Both were burrows in standing dead trees, one a *Pandanus* palm and the other an introduced *Albizzia*. Fledged young are still being fed by their parents in June.

The past distribution of the parrot is something of a mystery. Evidently it was once common all over Praslin, but there has never been a record from another island. Suitable palm forest habitat existed (and still survives in small patches) on Silhouette and in parts of Mahé, but on Mahé at least there was another parrot (the Green Parakeet, *Psittacula eupatria wardi*, now extinct) and perhaps the two did not coexist. The Black Parrot was, and occasionally still is, persecuted by man for raiding fruiting trees, especially mangoes; it seems to have adapted itself to the loss of the palm forests to the extent of finding other sources of food and other nesting sites. But the days when flocks of more than fifty were shot out of fruit trees are long since gone, despite the planters' stories, which are probably memories of times long ago. Now it is rare to see as many as a dozen birds together, and there may not be more than fifty individuals left. Most of the parrots roost in the Vallée de Mai, and during a dusk-to-dawn count by the Bristol Expedition in 1965 we accounted for only twenty-odd birds seen entering or leaving the Vallée.

The closest relatives of the Black Parrot are members of the same species, *Coracopsis n. nigra*, in Madagascar, and *C. n. sibilans* on Grand Comoro and Anjouan in the Comoros. Because of the long isolation of the species it is difficult to guess at its affinities to other *Coracopsis* species, for example *C. vasa*, which lives alongside *C. nigra* in Madagascar and on Anjouan and Grand Comoro.

GREEN PARAKEET   Cateau vert   *Psittacula eupatria wardi*
(Sey – extinct)   **Pl. 4**

The Seychelles Green Parakeet was slightly larger than the Black Parrot, green with a black collar in the male. It was last seen, and collected, on Mahé, in 1893 when it was said to be near to extinction there but common on Silhouette. In the 1860s there were said to be some on Praslin, but no ornithologist ever saw the species there. The forests of Silhouette are seldom visited, and the species might still survive there, but it seems very unlikely: the local people never mention it.

There are six skins in the Museum of Zoology at Cambridge, England, and three in the British Museum of Natural History in London; Harvard has two, the American Museum of Natural History has another, and there is at least one in Paris of the two collected by Lantz, the last ornithologist to see the bird alive.

The reasons for the extinction of the species are not clear, but probably persecution as a pest coupled with the destruction of habitat proved its downfall.

GREY-HEADED LOVEBIRD   Petit cateau vert
Agapornis cana   **Pl. 4**
Sey

A small pale green bird, lighter in colour below, with a grey head and neck in the male, and some grey on the breast; the female is green all over, paler on the head than on the wings. The voice is a subdued chatter most of the time, reminiscent of budgerigars, especially during the well-known courtship display which gives the bird its English name; a variety of squawks and whistles may be heard from a feeding flock.

Lovebirds are to be seen in Victoria early in the morning, and at all times at Port Launay, Anse la Mouche, and Anse Boileau. Elsewhere on the west coast of Mahé they may be seen from time to time. There is a small population on Silhouette, too, probably deliberately introduced. The diet is seeds, especially of 'Elephant Grass', *Panicum maximum*, which is grown in quantity in Seychelles to make *fataque* brooms. Flocks of up to fifty birds may be seen whirring about in the tall grass, or darting between coconut palms in a plantation.

The lovebird nests in holes in trees during the north-west monsoon, enlarging an opening in a rotten trunk or bough, and using the debris to line the nest. The eggs are white, usually three in number, less often two or four. Incubation and rearing of the young is shared by both sexes; the young birds are fed on regurgitated matter from the crop of the parent until they can fly at about four weeks, when they begin to eat seeds.

Lovebirds were introduced into Seychelles early in this century: at one time, during the 1930s, they were very common in Victoria, roosting in huge flocks all round Gordon Square; then they suffered an abrupt decline for reasons unknown, and now they are rare except in the three places mentioned above. Perhaps some disease carried them off, or perhaps it was the result of the declining fertility of an inbred population; at any rate the Government is not taking the chance of another parrot being established to the same extent, and the importation of breeding parrots is banned in the colony.

BARN OWL Hibou *Tyto alba affinis* Pl. 4
Sey

The introduced Barn Owl is much larger than the rare endemic Scops Owl; it is pale below and mottled chestnut and black above, the face distinguished by huge off-white facial discs

Plate 3   KESTRELS, PIGEONS AND DOVES

1. **Madagascar Kestrel** *Falco newtoni*   p. 61
   Bright chestnut above, streaked below. The only small bird of
   prey to be seen on Aldabra. Conspicuous and tame.

2. **Seychelles Kestrel** *Falco araea*   p. 62
   Dark chestnut above, plain below. Even smaller than Aldabra
   bird. Becoming scarce, but not uncommon in lowlands of
   Central Seychelles.

3. **Comoro Blue Pigeon** *Alectroenas sganzini minor*   p. 69
   Large blue and white pigeon, with conspicuous red surround
   to eye. Often in groups in fruiting trees. Aldabra.

4. **Seychelles Blue Pigeon** *Alectroenas pulcherrima*   p. 70
   Similar to **3**, but has convoluted red wattle in adult, larger in
   male. Juvenile greenish-brown, inconspicuous.

5. **Turtle Dove** *Streptopelia picturata*   p. 71
   Sturdy grey-blue doves, ground-feeding in open places.
   a, *S.p. picturata* Large, purplish mantle, *grey* head. Seychelles, Amirantes, and Chagos. Introduced from Madagascar.
   b, *S.p. rostrata* Smaller, chestnut mantle, *purple* head.
   Contaminated by **5a**, but phenotype still to be seen Cousin,
   Cousine, and Frigate.
   c, *S.p. coppingeri* Deep vinous purple all over upper parts.
   Aldabra.
   NOTE: *S.p. aldabrana,* a misnomer, is effectively extinct
   from the Amirantes, where it was once the endemic form.
   Turtle Doves seen in the Amirantes now should be assigned
   to *S.p. picturata.*

6. **Barred Ground Dove** *Geopelia striata*   p. 74
   Small light-brown dove with conspicuous blue eye-ring,
   long tail. Ground feeder, but may nest high up.

PARROT, PARAKEET, LOVEBIRD
AND OWLS

Plate 4

1. **Grey-headed Lovebird** *Agapornis cana*   p. 78
   Small pale-green lovebird. Mahé and Silhouette.
   a, Male: grey head and breast, otherwise green.
   b, Female: green all over, lighter below.

2. **Green Parakeet** *Psittacula eupatria wardi*   p. 78
   EXTINCT. Illustrated here from a skin in the Museum of
   Zoology, Cambridge, England. An example of what has been
   lost; not, to my knowledge, illustrated elsewhere.

3. **Black Parrot** *Coracopsis nigra barklyi*   p. 76
   Dark grey-brown, secretive. May be confused in flight with
   Blue Pigeon, but flies much faster and has bullet-headed
   look which is distinctive. Praslin only.

4. **Barn Owl** *Tyto alba affinis*   p. 79
   Large pale-coloured owl; conspicuous white facial discs.
   Call is a loud hiss, dusk and dawn.

5. **Seychelles Bare-legged Scops Owl** *Oths insularis*   q. 83
   Small size, darker colour, rasping voice distinguish from
   Barn Owl. Very rare; mountains of Mahé and possibly
   Praslin.

NOTE: The Fairy Tern shown as the prey of the Barn Owl
has the typical blue bill of adults, not visible in the Mono-
chrome Plate 12.

surrounding the large eyes. (This appearance earns it its American name of 'Monkey-faced Owl'.) The voice is a loud harsh hiss, sometimes given on the wing as well as from a perch. In the breeding season the call is more vocalised, almost a scream, and there is a peculiar 'yodelling' call which I have heard in the early morning.

Barn Owls are found on all the granitic islands of any size, including Cousin and especially Cousine. They may be seen at night in the headlamps of a car, sitting on bare branches above the mountain roads; and their calls may be heard from the seashore to the tops of the hills. Their diet is small birds, including sunbirds, fodies, and the young of doves and pigeons. They specialise in eating Fairy Terns, which are, of course, very conspicuous at night, to the extent that the terns are nearly extinct on Mahé and Praslin, and not much more common on La Digue. Very occasionally a small rat or a lizard is taken, judging from the analysis of a large number of pellets by the Bristol Expedition.

The nest is in a cleft in rocks, often in church towers, occasionally even in coconut palms. The eggs are rather small and round, white or dirty pale brown in colour, the clutch six to eight. One nest on Praslin had thirteen eggs in it, but it was probably being shared by two females. The young are grotesque until they develop the facial discs; they are covered in greyish-white down, with large feet and long bills, conspicuous until the normal plumage develops. There are usually young of different ages in the nest, since the eggs are incubated from the day of laying and hatch serially, each in about thirty-three days. This is typical of owls and a few other birds; it permits the fledging of a large clutch in times of plenty, but in hard times the older chicks kill and eat the younger, for whom there is no food. From my experience on Cousin, where we conducted a continuous campaign against owls, the breeding season is continuous, too.

Barn Owls were introduced to Ile Platte from East Africa in 1949 as an 'experiment' to see if they could control rats. Amid a plethora of rats, they died out. The Department of Agriculture, nothing daunted, introduced more in 1951 and 1952, this time to Mahé. This time they succeeded in establishing the species, and for twelve years the owls rampaged unchecked through the endemic avifauna. Needless to say, the rats were hardly touched, though from time to time the skeleton of one would be found in an owl's nest, and hailed as a breakthrough. After much acrimonious debate, and partly as the result of the evidence collected by the Bristol Expedition, the owl was finally convicted of killing birds rather than rats, and a price was put on its head. The bounty on owls is now thirty rupees, and there is some hope that this will cause some reduction in their numbers, but to wipe them out altogether will be impossible.

You might have a soft spot for owls in general, but if you find a nest, just pick up one or two of the pellets lying about, and look at the pathetic small bones there. Then you will feel able to put a quick and humane end to any Barn Owl you can catch.

Barn Owls of the same race were common on Aldabra in 1893 when Abbott was there, and one was collected in 1906, but they have not been seen since. The reason for their extinction is not apparent, but it might have been competition from the (newly established?) kestrel. These owls, of course, must have arrived by natural means.

SEYCHELLES BARE-LEGGED SCOPS OWL Scieur
Otus insularis   **Pl. 4**
Sey

A small buff-coloured owl, with speckled wings and bright yellow eyes, the Seychelles Scops Owl differs from African Scops Owls in having only small ear-tufts, and bare legs. On account of this last feature it used to be in a genus of its own, *Gymnoscops*. The voice of the Scops Owl is what gives it its Créole name: a slow, rhythmic rasping like that of a saw, interspersed with 'tok tok' noises like a sawyer knocking in a wedge. It is not yet known whether these calls are both produced by the same bird or by the members of a pair.

The Scops Owl is now restricted to sites high in the mountains of Mahé, but it has been heard in the last couple of years in at least three different places; it is almost certainly still to be found at Point Cabri on Praslin; and there is some evidence that it survives also on Félicité. It was probably always a forest bird, but before man came to the islands its habitat would have included the lower slopes of the mountains and even the lowlands. As the forest was removed from these places the owl retreated into the hills, where on calm clear nights its calls are still to be heard. The diet is unknown, but one would expect it to consist of large insects, tree frogs, and lizards.

The nest has never been seen. Probably a cleft in the rocks, at a guess containing three or four white eggs (assuming that the clutch of this insular species would be smaller than that of Scops Owls in Africa), it would have to be in a high and little frequented part of the forest, perhaps on the face of one of those daunting precipices above Victoria. The Bristol Expedition surprised a Scops Owl in daylight at Castor in 1965, but were unable to find the nest.

The Scops Owl was presumed extinct from 1906 until 1959, when Philippe Lalanne saw one in the mountains of South Mahé. There is a skin in the British Museum which was collected in 1940, but that came to light after Lalanne's discovery. To foresters and charcoal burners – and to one tea planter of my acquaintance – its call has always been a familiar sound at night, but ornithologists have had bad luck in locating the bird. Roger Tory Peterson saw the owl in 1970, the first record since ours of 1965, and not for lack of looking. If not the rarest, this is surely the least often seen of all the birds of Seychelles. A photograph of one shot by mistake is published in *Animals* for May, 1972.

The genus *Otus* is widespread in East Africa; the nearest relative to our species is *O. rutilus* of the Comoros, but there is nothing very close, suggesting that the Seychelles species has been isolated for a very long time.

SEYCHELLES CAVE SWIFTLET Hirondelle
Collocalia francica elaphra **Pl. 5**
Sey

The Cave Swiftlet is a small dark swallow-like bird, distinguished from the species in the Mascarenes by its overall darkness – greyish brown, lighter below – and by the lack of a white patch on the rump. The voice is a soft twitter, sometimes heard from a group of birds on the wing; within their nesting cave they use an echo-location call, a regular low-pitched 'pewterpewter', extraordinarily metallic, almost electronic, in character.

Swiftlets are to be seen almost anywhere on the larger islands, high over the mountain forests or swooping low across swampy ground or pools, in pursuit of their prey. They feed in the manner common to their kind, on small insects taken on the wing.

The nest was first discovered by John Procter in 1970, in a cave underneath a boulder ruckle on the slope of Nid d'Aigles, La Digue. There were two groups of nests, twenty-two in all, attached to the ceiling of the cave. They are bracket shaped, made of a lichen mixed with the sticky saliva of the birds, in one group attached to a 45° reverse slope, in the other on the horizontal ceiling. Marks on the walls round about indicated that this site has been in use for a long time, and there were huge piles of droppings under the next to emphasise this. In July the colony had two single white eggs on the 5th, and four or more ten days later. The clutch in the Mascarenes is two, but in Seychelles it is one only – as we should expect from an insular race. In Seychelles the breeding season is evidently at the beginning of the south-east monsoon, but in the Mascarenes it is in December. There, too, the birds breed in large colonies; the colony on La Digue was small, but perhaps it was not typical.

The swiftlet seems not to have suffered from the attentions of man – even from the Chinese community and their soup cauldrons – probably because its nesting site is so inaccessible and its diet so easily supplied.

MADAGASCAR NIGHTJAR Sommeil *Caprimulgus*
madagascariensis aldabrensis   **Pl. 5**
Ald

This is a large typical nightjar, the colour of dead leaves, with
white (male) or golden (female) patches on wings and tail, a
huge mouth and large lustrous eyes. The voice is a rattling sound,
'Tyok-ok-k-k-k-k', rather like a knife being thrown into a board.
Single 'tyok!' calls are also heard, and sometimes a fluty 'huuuu'
call preceding the call proper.

The nightjar is inconspicuous, like all its family, but it may be
quite common at Aldabra. Certainly it is heard all over the atoll
at night, except apparently during the non-breeding season.
The birds lie up during the day under bushes, when they are
very hard to find except by chance; once discovered, however,
they are quite tame. They are more common in open country
than in the dense bush, as would be expected, since their feeding
habits require room to manoeuvre. They feed on the wing,
hawking silently low over the ground, taking large insects such
as *Mantis* and *Cicada*, as well as many nocturnal beetles.

The nest is a mere scrape on bare ground, a shallow depression
in which the one or two mottled eggs are laid. Against the usual
background of small gravel and litter the egg is almost invisible.
Both parents attend the nest during incubation, but beyond that
almost nothing is known of the breeding behaviour. The season
seems to be from September to December, when the calls are
most frequently heard.

The nightjar does not seem to be under pressure at Aldabra,
though it might suffer somewhat from the attentions of rats,
laying its eggs on the ground. A tame cat caught a nightjar at
the Settlement during the Royal Society Expedition – the skin
of the bird is in the British Museum, but history does not relate
what became of the cat – and feral cats must be something of a
threat as well; but on the whole the nightjar seems to be quite
common, protected by its extremely cryptic colouring.

The closest relative is the Madagascar Nightjar, nominate
madagascariensis, which is exactly the same size, but darker in

colour. Nightjars have not been recorded from other islands in the group.

MADAGASCAR BULBUL Merle *Hypsipetes*
madagascariensis rostratus   Pl. 5
Ald

The bulbul is a small scruffy grey-brown bird with a black erectile crest and a bright orange bill; juveniles have a dull brown bill and rusty edges to the flight feathers. The voice is a series of ringing whistles on two notes, heard usually in the evening, and harsh chattering alarm and combat cries. The alarm call when a bird is disturbed is a single harsh screech, repeated endlessly from a perch, a most annoying sound.

The bulbul is common all over Aldabra, especially in the open bushy country, where parties of two and three barge about through the vegetation, chattering and fighting. Occasionally there are 'jamborees' of twenty or more birds in the evening, giving vent to penetrating whistles and squawks. In the dark woodland at Takamaka Grove the bulbuls surround an intruder, calling loudly. They are omnivorous, taking fruits and insects equally often, as well as the buds of flowering shrubs. One flew across my camp site at Takamaka one evening carrying in its bill a *Cicada* which was still stridulating.

The breeding season is the first part of the north-west monsoon, from October to December. The nest is a neat cup in a sheltered site, the clutch two speckled eggs. Adults have been seen feeding young away from the nest in January, but apart from that record little is known of the breeding behaviour; for all its conspicuous behaviour at other times, the bulbul is secretive about its nesting activities.

Bulbuls are not recorded from other islands in the Aldabra group – for the Seychelles species see page 88 – and they probably never occurred there. At Aldabra they appear to be practically unaffected by man, and with the white-eye and the sunbird they are among the most abundant land bird species.

They are not as confiding as the cardinal around houses, but they are tame in the bush. They seem to have no enemies.

The nearest relatives are two other members of the same species: *H. m. parvirostris* of the Comoros, and *H. m. madagascariensis* of Madagascar; *rostratus* is equally distinct from both, and its origins are not clear.

SEYCHELLES BULBUL   Merle   *Hypsipetes*
crassirostris crassirostris   **Pl. 5**
Sey

Similar in appearance to its Aldabra cousin, but larger, more heavily built and greenish, the Seychelles Bulbul is one of the endemic birds of the granitic islands which does not seem to have suffered from the arrival of man. The voice of the Seychelles bird is similar to the Aldabra species, with whistles and hoarse shrieks, but the Seychelles bird also imitates other birds with great accuracy. On Praslin it can deceive one into looking about for Black Parrots, and on all the islands it uses mynah calls as well. Since the mynah is also imitative, this produces a rather confused situation! Generally, however, the two can be separated by ear because the bulbul cannot produce the power of the mynah's whistle, and the mynah does not have the characteristic hoarse component in its vocabulary.

Bulbuls are not common in the town, or indeed anywhere in the lowlands of Mahé, though they may be seen there; but everywhere else they are abundant and conspicuous, especially in the evenings as they squabble at the roost. Their diet is chiefly berries and insects, but they are omnivorous around houses.

The nest is a neat round cup built in October or November into the fork of a tree. Moss and spider's web in the lower levels give way to grass and palm fibres higher up, and finer grass is used as a lining. Both sexes share in the building at first, but as the sides of the nest rise one bird (probably the female, though the sexes are indistinguishable) stays on the nest assembling the material brought by the other. The site is usually above head height, and nests have been found as much as forty feet above the ground. Two eggs are laid, pinkish ivory in ground colour with numerous brown spots and blotches. The chicks are hideous, bald and helpless, and the parents take it in turn to brood them for the first few days until the down begins to sprout. The young birds fly after three weeks, at first staying with their parents and begging occasional meals from them until they are repulsed and have to fend for themselves.

The bulbul is inquisitive, approaching rather than fleeing a stranger in the forest, but presumably because it is not supposed to be good to eat it has not suffered for this tameness in the same way as other birds like the Blue Pigeon. Apart from its absence from the town, its distribution now must be very similar to what it was before men came; more common in the forest, but pretty abundant everywhere.

The Seychelles Bulbul is aberrant in several ways, apart from being large and dull-coloured, as we have come to expect from island birds. The whole genus *Hypsipetes* has stronger flight than other bulbuls, which tend to be inhabitants of dense thickets rather than the more open forests in which *Hypsipetes* has evolved. Also, being a forest genus, our bulbul builds its nest higher up than the others. A minor point but another oddity is that it uses moss in its nests, unlike the other bulbuls. The Seychelles Bulbul (sometimes called the Thick-billed Bulbul) is found only here and on one of the Comoros (*H. c. moheliensis*). It shares this peculiar distribution with the Chestnut-flanked White-eye, which is extinct in Seychelles but survives on Mayotte in the Comoros, and occurs nowhere else. On Moheli in the Comoros the Thick-billed Bulbul coexists with the Malagasy Bulbul, *H. madagascariensis*, which is found also on Aldabra. A third species in the area is *H. borbonicus*, which has diverged on Mauritius and Réunion. All *Hypsipetes* are ancestrally Asian.

SEYCHELLES MAGPIE ROBIN   Pie chanteuse
Copsychus sechellarum   **Pl. 6**
Sey

Although it is black and white and carries its tail cocked, this charming bird is neither a magpie nor a robin. It is in fact a member of the thrush family, of a genus which is widespread in Asia. The adults are entirely black with a blue sheen, save for a clear white patch on the upper half of the wing. Young birds have the wing patch fringed with chestnut markings, and lack the sheen of adults. The voice is a quiet disjointed little song much of the time, with occasional virtuoso performances in the evenings during the breeding season.

The Magpie Robin is found now only on Frigate Island, in the east of the granitic group. It is most commonly seen around the houses, bounding round in search of scraps, and in the few remaining patches of woodland, where it loves to sit in deep shade. Its diet away from the settlement includes termites and giant millipedes, but round the houses it will eat anything. The inhabitants of Frigate have a kindly disposition towards the birds, and often throw out rice for them to feed on – which has made them even more tame than they were when the early bird collectors recorded how easy it was to knock Magpie Robins down with sticks.

    The nest is rarely seen: it is built in the top of coconut palms, in the bowl-shaped bases of the fronds, an untidy jumble of bits of vegetation with a neat cup in the middle. The clutch is usually two pale blue eggs, but the incubation time and fledging period are not known. The family group stays together after the young birds have fledged; during the Bristol Expedition we saw a pair with young of widely differing ages in April. The breeding season seems to extend from November to March at least, and it is possible that a pair might breed twice in the season. The only description of the courtship was written by Philippe Lalanne, who watched it in November. He mentions drooping wings and tail in the male, and the bill pointed to the sky, with hoarse calls to the female, who sits still, fluffed out, while the male hops round her.

In the past the Magpie Robin was on Mahé (1867 the last record there), Praslin (last seen after the war and perhaps into the fifties), La Digue, Marianne, and Félicité. Apart from the possibility that it might still survive in some remote part of Praslin, it is extinct on all these islands now. As a tame ground-feeding bird, it was easy meat for introduced cats and rats; it was nearly wiped out on Frigate by feral cats, until a concentrated cat-drive reduced their numbers to an insignificant level. A population of introduced Magpie Robins on Alphonse in the Amirantes was flourishing so well in 1940 that Vesey-Fitzgerald called that island the 'last stronghold' of the species; but when we searched Alphonse in 1965 there was not one Magpie Robin to be seen, and none of the plantation staff could recall seeing one for six years or more. Now the sole survivors are probably the birds on Frigate, which number between thirty and forty. There is some evidence that this tiny population is increasing under the greater protection which it now receives. Nevertheless, if Frigate is ever developed for the tourist trade, great care must be taken not to wipe out the Magpie Robin.

Magpie Robins are a south-east Asian group of birds, also found in Madagascar, where some of the avifauna is Asian in origin rather than African. The Seychelles species is probably an offshoot from the Malagasy population, but it has diverged so far that we cannot tell for certain where it came from. All the other Magpie Robins, with the exception of an oddity in the East Indies, are ginger and black and white, and small; the Seychelles species is a prime example of an insular derivative, being very large, and very dark in colour. Its ancestral colouring is revealed only in the gingery wing-patches of the young birds.

ALDABRA BRUSH WARBLER *Nesillas aldabranus* **Pl. 5**
Ald

A new species, discovered by the Royal Society Expedition to Aldabra in 1967 (see Benson and Penny, 1968). It is a dingy dark brown bird, white below with a very long tail, easily distinguished from the Grass Warbler, *Cisticola cherina*, by its laage size, and even rather than streaky colouring. Its song has never been heard, but its call is a three-syllable nasal chirrup.

The Brush Warbler – sometimes known by the Malagasy name Tskirity – is a very rare skulking bird, and has been seen only by half a dozen people. It lives in the dense *Pemphis* thicket at the western end of Middle Island, more than ten miles of which has never been penetrated by man. We have no idea how many there might be, but evidently it was not more widespread when the early collectors were visiting Aldabra, or they would have seen it. Its diet is insectivorous, including moths, beetles, and caterpillars.

The first nest found was in the leaf bases of a *Pandanus* shrub; two others nearby were higher up, in the thin branches of small trees. The construction was the same in all, shredded *Pandanus* leaves with a lining of fine grass. The only clutch seen was three pinkish speckled eggs in December. All three nests were apparently of the same season.

The distribution of the species is not known further than I have indicated above: no one has ever been able to penetrate the *Pemphis* in search of further birds. There is another huge impenetrable area of the same kind of bush at the west end of South Island, where the species may also occur. It is difficult to imagine what natural enemies the bird might have; the first nest site would have been protected from rats by the spines of the *Pandanus*.

N. aldabranus is closely related to the group of *N. typica* subspecies in Madagascar, being most like *N. t. lantzii* of the dry south-west. This similarity is probably parallel evolution rather than any evidence of relationship, since it is well known that birds of dry climates tend to be pale in colour. The distinction of *N. aldabranus* is held to be specific because of the much greater length of its bill and tail. The relation between *Nesillas* and the Brush Warblers, *Bebrornis*, of Seychelles and Rodriguez is not at all clear.

SEYCHELLES BRUSH WARBLER Petit Merle des Iles
Bebrornis seychellensis **Pl. 5**
Sey

The Seychelles Brush Warbler is of much the same build as the Aldabra bird, a long-tailed long-billed warbler; its colour is much more greenish, the under parts creamy and slightly streaked in some individuals. The long slender legs are grey-blue in colour. The voice is a rich melodious song, reminiscent of an English blackbird or an American robin; the alarm call is a brisk chatter. Juveniles utter a wheezy squeak over and again, until they are silenced by the parental alarm.

The Brush Warbler is found now only on the small island of Cousin – though Tony Beamish saw in 1970 one survivor of six birds introduced to Cousine in about 1960 – and the island was bought and established as a sanctuary principally for the sake of the warbler. It lives in the dense scrub which has grown up in the old coconut plantation, and in the swamp on the south side of the island. It is insectivorous, taking small flying insects on the wing as well as beetles and spiders from among the vegetation. The crisp 'clack' of its bill as it seizes its prey is often the first sign of its presence. Evidently it is not exclusively an insect-eater, however, for a warbler has been known to take a very small baby skink from the ground.

The nest of the warbler is neat and sturdy, like the bird. It is built into a fragile fork, usually just below the canopy of the bush, made of coconut fibres and grass, lined with finer material, but any convenient materials may be used, including cotton rags or wood shavings from round the house, and in one case a whole polythene bag, from which the birds seemed to suffer no ill effects. The breeding season is not properly known, but it seems that the birds breed every eight months regardless of season; work is still going on to clarify this. There are sometimes two eggs, but one is the usual clutch; the egg is ivory in colour, with numerous green and brown speckles – not reddish as in the Malagasy and Aldabra birds. The chick hatches in about fifteen days, and leaves the nest very soon afterwards, long before it can fly. It is very agile at scrambling among the branches at this early age, however, and it seems likely that to leave so soon is a defence against the lizards which are very common on Cousin, which would rob the nest. The parents locate the wandering juvenile by its continuous hoarse cries. Both parents feed the chick, not only until it is fledged but long afterwards, almost up to the pair's next breeding season. During this time the chick is well able to forage for itself, but it continues to solicit food from the parents, perhaps as a means of maintaining its position as a dependent and thus avoiding being expelled from the parental territory until the latest possible moment.

The warbler was first described by Oustalet in 1877, from a specimen collected by Lantz on Marianne, where the species is now extinct. Lantz reported that it was 'rare on Ile Cousine', but this might have been a mistake for Cousin. There are no records from any other island in the group, though presumably it occurred at one time at least on Praslin. The estimated population of Cousin during the breeding period in June, 1970, was eighty-five birds, including the season's young; this might be as many as the island can support, because of the strictly territorial nature of the pairs. The frequency of breeding must mean that the territories are maintained for a large part of the year, leaving the young birds a very short period of grace in which to find a territory of their own between breeding periods. Work is still going on into the way in which the birds have adjusted to the shortage of space, but one thing that is clear is that their clutch size is lower than that of related birds in more spacious surroundings. As more of the scrub grows up in the old plantation on Cousin there might be a few more territories; but the future of the species depends on the continued protection of the island.

The nearest relative to the Seychelles Brush Warbler is the Rodriguez species, *Bebrornis rodericana*. Both are close in shape and colour to the brush warblers of Madagascar, Aldabra, and the Comoros; but these are usually placed in the separate genus, *Nesillas*, because the *Bebrornis* species are too different for anyone to be quite certain that they came from the same ancestral stock, though it seems likely. There is no African or Indian warbler now to which these birds seem to be closely related, and so the question must be left open.

Continuing research into the origins and population balance of the Seychelles Brush Warbler might one day answer questions about small isolated populations elsewhere.

MALAGASY GRASS WARBLER *Cisticola cherina* Pl. 5
Cos Ast

A small dingy warbler, streaky above with very dark brown on mid-brown, and pale below, almost white. Males have the top of the head evenly coloured dark brown, and females and non-breeding birds are more streaky both on the head and the back. Voice when alarmed a crisp 'tic' rather like an English robin; the courtship song a drawn-out version of the same call, repeated every second or so – 'tzeec . . . tzeec'.

The Malagasy Grass Warbler is common on Cosmoledo and Astove, but absent from other islands in the area. It is most often seen among the herbs growing in the scrub on those islands, but it is also to be found in the dunes and around the settlements. It is insectivorous, feeding mostly low down among grass and in small cover.

In the breeding season, which seems to extend from October through to April or even later, the males are more conspicuous, performing their courtship flight above the cover; the rest of the time both sexes skulk and are not easy to see. The nest is typical of the genus, a domed affair of grass with the entrance hole high up in the side; there are three spotted eggs, ivory with reddish markings. The nest is usually only a couple of inches off the ground among grass stems, but on Cosmoledo one was found as much as two feet up, perhaps as a defence against rats.

The grass warbler seems to be a recent invader of the two islands, the first real record being in 1940, away from its home in Madagascar. Benson quotes a possible record of Bergne in 1907 from Cosmoledo, but the species concerned is defined only by the Créole name 'allouette', which, although it means 'lark' –

Plate 5   SWIFTLET, NIGHTJAR, BULBUL,
WARBLERS AND FLYCATCHER

1. **Seychelles Cave Swiftlet**   *Collocalia francica elaphra*   p. 85
Small, dark, swallow-like bird. Uniform dark colour, hardly
paler below, distinguishes from (larger) vagrant Hirundines.
Nests as illustrated, in caves at base of mountains among
boulders.

2. **Madagascar Bulbul**   *Hypsipetes madagascariensis rostratus*   p. 87
Dark grey-brown bird with orange bill, black erectile crest.
Aldabra.

3. **Seychelles Bulbul**   *Hypsipetes crassirostris crassirostris*   p. 88
Dark grey-brown bird with black crest as **2.** Calls may
imitate Mynah or Black Parrot (Praslin).

4. **Seychelles Black Paradise Flycatcher**   *Terpsiphone*   p. 98
La Digue only.   *corvina*
a, Male: black all over with deep blue sheen; long tail plumes
in breeding dress. Blue bill and facial skin.
b, Female: chestnut on wings, whitish breast. Head as male
but lacks facial skin colouring.

5. **Aldabra Brush Warbler**   *Nesillas aldabranus*   p. 91
Similar to Seychelles species (below), but drabber in colour
and with longer tail. From Middle Island, Aldabra.

6. **Seychelles Brush Warbler**   *Bebrornis seychellensis*   P. 93
Greenish-yellow warbler. Slender bill and delicate colouring
distinguish it from weavers on Cousin. Cousin Island, but
one report from Cousine 1970.

7. **Madagascar Nightjar**   *Caprimulgus madagascariensis*   p. 86
                                          aldabrensis
Unmistakeable dead-leaf-coloured bird. Roosts on ground
in daytime. Male, illustrated, has white wing-patches and
tail corners: female has golden beige in these places.

8. **Malagasy Grass Warbler**   *Cisticola cherina*   p. 95
Small dingy warbler, streaky above, pale below; females
more streaky than males. Cosmoledo and Astove.

COUCAL, MAGPIE ROBIN, DRONGO, CROW AND MYNAH Plate 6

1. **Madagascar Coucal** *Centropus toulou insularis*   p. 75
Large skulking bird in dense cover; secretive except when singing.
a, Non-breeding: streaky brown with whitish spots. Sexes alike. Aldabra, but may also occur at Assumption.
b, Breeding dress: glossy black with chestnut wings.

2. **Aldabra Drongo** *Dicrurus aldabranus*   p. 100
Sits upright on perch. Deeply forked tail distinctive.
a, Juveniles dingy grey above, streaky whitish below.
b, Adults shiny black all over.

3. **Indian Mynah** *Acridotheres tristis*   p. 103
Brownish with black head and yellow facial skin and bill. Calls may imitate Parrot (Praslin) or Bulbul. Rare mutant has bald yellow head and black neck.
a, Flying: note white in tail, smaller wing patches than Magpie Robin, and brown on back.
b, Perched on ground.

4. **Seychelles Magpie Robin** *Copsychus sechellarum*   p. 90
Black, thrush-like bird with white wing patches. Juveniles lack adults' blue sheen; have faint ginger freckles in wing-patch. Frigate only.
a, Flying: note lack of white in tail, large wing patches, and compare with 3a.
b, Perched on ground.

5. **Pied Crow** *Corvus albus*   p. 101
Large, conspicuous, black and white crow. Scavenges around human habitation.

B.S.   G

and the grass warbler looks quite like a lark – is used by the Seychellois as a generic term for small waders, such as Curlew Sandpipers, not for passerines. There seems to be no Créole name for this species, but something like 'serin' or 'moineau' would be more likely.

The genus *Cisticola* is very widespread, ranging to Australia, but nearly all the species are African. This one in particular seems to be most closely related to the very widespread *C. juncidis*.

SEYCHELLES BLACK PARADISE FLYCATCHER
Veuve   *Terpsiphone corvina*   **Pl. 5**
Sey

Long black tail streamers, a pale blue bill, and black plumage with a deep blue sheen make the male flycatcher quite unmistakable. The female is more brightly coloured, with the head the same as that of the male, chestnut wings and tail, and creamy white underparts. She lacks the tail streamers of the male, and is much less conspicuous in flight; she also lacks the pale blue strip of facial skin between the male's eye and bill. Both sexes are about the size of a sparrow. The voice of the male is a piping whistle on a rising note, repeated several times, rather like a man calling a dog. The Seychellois interpret this as a sign of rain – 'pli pli pli pli'. The female has a very quiet twittering voice, seldom heard.

The veuve is found to our knowledge only on La Digue, though there have recently been rumours that it might still survive in quiet parts of Praslin. On La Digue it lives in the lowland woods round the main settlement, where in the darkness of the vanilla groves and the Badamier woods its twisting flight is hard to follow. During the south-east monsoon, however, the males are much more conspicuous, as they indulge in fierce aerial combat over the boundaries of territories. The diet of the veuve is insects, caught on the wing or picked from leaves – hence its preference for the damp shady woods of La Digue, which are full of insects.

The breeding season starts in about September with the territorial battles, and proceeds through the north-west monsoon until April or even later. The nest is built on a slender down-hanging branch of Badamier (as a rule, though, Takamaka and even *Casuarina* may be used), a neat cup solidly bound with spider's web. The materials are palm fibres and *Casuarina* needles, lined with finer materials such as grass. One egg is the rule, though two have occasionally been found; both sexes incubate, the returning bird relieving the other with a delightful twittering song. This is the only time in the breeding cycle when the female does not exert her dominance over the male; during nest-building, and to a greater extent later, during the feeding of the young, the male is completely subordinate to the female, fleeing the nest when she approaches even though he was on the point of feeding the chick. One female chased a male away from a nest with a chick for a distance of some fifty yards before she would feed the chick. The male returned after the female had left, to feed the chick surreptitiously himself. The chick fledges in a juvenile plumage which is very like that of the female, though less brightly coloured; it is not until the next moult that the young bird assumes the distinctive clothing of its sex.

The veuve was last recorded on Curieuse in 1906, and on Félicité as late as 1936, but it is extinct there now. Some people say that it still occurs on Praslin, but the latest record of the bird there which sounds at all authentic was in 1945–50 at Grand' Anse. However, it would be well worth searching among the woods behind the plantation at Anse Kerlan and round that north-west corner of Praslin.

The reasons for the decline of the veuve are surely the loss of the shady woodland which it needs both for feeding and nesting, coupled with an increase in human population. The importance of the latter point can be appreciated when the nesting site is considered: the bird nests near a clearing, giving it easy access to the nest, and plenty of warning of the approach of danger. The narrow twig on which the nest is suspended protects it from lizards, which must have been a major enemy of the species in the past. Now the clearing is a house-yard or a path as often as not, and on the densely crowded island of La Digue nests may be destroyed when coconuts are cut down, or when a carelessly carried headload knocks them off the branch, or even when a bored child sees them as a challenging target for a catapult. As a result of all this, the veuve is probably the most endangered species in Seychelles. However, the Government has recently appointed a warden on La Digue whose sole responsibility is to look after the bird, and the inhabitants are beginning to realise the honour as well as the financial value of having their own island bird, so that there is hope yet.

The genus *Terpsiphone* is very widespread: it occurs virtually all over Africa south of the Sahara, and over much of southern Asia, as well as in the Mascarenes. The nearest relative to the Seychelles species is *T. mutata*, which has a subspecies in Madagascar, and four in the Comoros, one on each of the major islands.

ALDABRA DRONGO   Moulin ban   *Dicrurus aldabranus*
Ald   Pl. 6

The drongo is most noticeable for the way in which it sits on a branch; it has a very upright posture, the long deeply forked tail projecting vertically below the perch. The bird is black all over, with a brownish sheen, and a very heavy bill which gives the head a wedge-shaped appearance. Young birds are dingy grey above and white below, rather streaky, but the same distinctive shape as the adults. The voice is nasal and metallic, especially in the nest-defending chant, 'titi-po fa fa'.* There is a variety of other squawks, and also a gentle muttering sound uttered during courtship.

The drongo is generally distributed on all four islands of Aldabra, not elsewhere in the group, but it is nowhere common. Most frequent sightings are in and near the mangroves on the south

*The attack call of the African Drongo is an inversion of this: 'fa-fa titi-poo'!

side of the lagoon and along the edge of Middle Island. The diet is insects of all sizes, up to cicadas, and also small geckoes. There is some suggestion that the drongo might also prey on the young of other birds, or even eat its own young at times of stress. It is extremely fierce in the defence of its nesting territory, driving off pied crows and even herons without hesitation.

The breeding season is from October or November through to December, a rather limited period compared with most other birds on the atoll. The nest is a sturdy cup, very strongly woven out of grass and woodrush, usually on a slender branch of a mangrove or other tree near water, but once at least on a branch overhanging a solution hole, so that it was actually below ground level. The clutch is two or three eggs, large, cream-coloured with reddish and black speckles at the large end. It seems that not all the eggs hatch, since some family parties contain only one young bird. While the nest is in use the adults are very fierce in its defence, actually striking a human observer who comes too close; but during building they are very shy, and will abandon a half-built nest at the slightest disturbance.

The drongo has few if any enemies which could do it any harm, in view of its valour in defending its nest; it seems that its relative scarcity at Aldabra might be due to the extremely territorial behaviour of breeding birds, which must exclude young birds from establishing themselves.

The drongo's nearest relative is clearly *D. forficatus* of Madagascar, from which the Aldabra species is most markedly differentiated by the unusual colour of the young, which in all other species are as black as their parents. The Aldabra Drongo also has an unusually large bill, the product of its insular evolution. *Dicrurus* is an African and Asiatic genus. The drongo, with the newly discovered brush warbler, is one of the only two full species of bird peculiar to Aldabra.

PIED CROW Corbeau *Corvus albus* **Pl. 6**
Ast *Cos* *Ass* **Ald**

The Pied Crow, an African species, is a large unmistakable

black and white bird, commonly seen round the settlements of the islands in the Aldabra group and Astove. Its voice is typically crow-like – a harsh 'caahnk' given in alarm, or a low-pitched gurgling heard from courting birds.

Aldabra seems to be the centre of the small population in the outer islands, and round the fish-racks at Settlement the crow is quite common. Elsewhere on the atoll it is scarce, though there is a small breeding group at Cinq Cases; but as soon as a fishing camp is occupied for more than a few days the crows move in, coming from Settlement Island in search of food. Their diet is omnivorous and scavenging, especially on the corpses of tortoises or turtles which are to be found on the dunes along the south coast, and of course on fish offal and drying fish on the settlement. From the fact that the crows are mobbed by drongos and kestrels, one might infer that they are also predatory, perhaps on the young of other birds; they have certainly been seen to take the eggs of noddies, Bridled Terns, and boobies.

The breeding season of the Pied Crow at Aldabra seems to be November to January, though in the Comoros and in south central Africa it starts earlier. The soaring courtship flight may be seen at Aldabra from October on, and nests have been found in November. The nest is built high up, in a coconut palm or a *Casuarina* tree, an untidy bundle of large twigs. The clutch size is not known for Aldabra, but it is not likely to be different from the mainland clutch, most usually four to six eggs.

Crows have been recorded at Aldabra since 1895, but the first breeding record was not until 1967, by the Royal Society Expedition. It is suggested that the Pied Crow is a recent arrival to the atoll, probably since man came; there may not be more than 100 birds all told, and in such a small colony breeding might be only sporadic. The crow depends for its livelihood on the activities of man. Records from the other islands are few and far between, but the species was seen on Astove, where it might breed, and Cosmoledo and Assumption, in 1967.

There is no geographical variation between the crows of Aldabra and those of the mainland, confirming the idea that their spread to the islands has been recent; they are strongly flighted birds, and can move at least from Aldabra to Assumption under their own power: but possibly they arrived in the islands as passengers on ships. Frazier has observed crows soaring high on updraughts over the islands, and this habit could make it easier for them to move from one island to another.

INDIAN MYNAH Martin *Acridotheres tristis* Pl. 6
Sey

Mynahs are conspicuous birds, black with a bold yellow face-patch and clear white bars on the wing and across the end of the tail which are visible only in flight; the back is brown. The voice of the mynah is loud and shrill, with a variety of piercing calls, especially in the early morning and at dusk; it also mimics other birds, such as the bulbul and the Black Parrot. Very occasionally a mutant form of mynah is seen, in which the entire head and neck are bald, the head yellow and the neck black. This is called by local people 'Le Roi Martin'.

The mynah is the most common and conspicuous bird of the lowlands of the larger islands, and some way into the hills. It does not breed on Cousin or Cousine, nor, I believe, on Aride. It is omnivorous, a successful scavenger round human habitations, which is doubtless one of the reasons for its success in the islands where it has been introduced. It is also predatory on the eggs and chicks of smaller birds; one took a Fairy Tern chick almost from under its mother's feet. Occasionally mynahs are to be seen 'playing Cattle Egrets', catching flies disturbed by the movements of cattle.

The nest is a loose scruffy bundle of grass and twigs, often in the roof of a building, or a coconut palm; the eggs, two or three in number, are rather small, and blue. The incubation period is about fifteen days, and both parents share the tasks of hatching and rearing the young.

The mynah is said to have been introduced in the late eighteenth century – soon after the first colonisation – by Mahé

de Labourdonnais, who arranged for the birds to be sent from
Mauritius, where they had been introduced from India to
control locusts. Locusts are almost unknown in Seychelles,
probably not because the mynah was a wild success, but because
of the isolation of the islands; it seems most likely that it was
really introduced here, as elsewhere in the world, as a cage bird
whose mimicry made it an entertaining pet.

SOUIMANGA SUNBIRD   Colibri   *Nectarinia sovimanga* subspp.   **Pl. 7**
Ald   Cos-Ast   Ass

A drab sunbird by African standards, the Souimanga Sunbird is
nevertheless the brightest among the islands. The male has a
metallic green head and neck, a red chest band, and yellow
pectoral tufts, visible under the wings in display. The female
lacks the decorative features, being dark grey-brown above and
grey-white below. The flight call of both sexes is a brisk chirrup,
given at the peaks of the looping flight; song is confined to the
male, a complex series of trills, rising and falling, but repeated in
a recognisable pattern which may be individually distinct for
each bird. Both sexes have a loud single-note alarm call.

The sunbird is very common in all parts of Aldabra, including
the mangroves, and the local subspecies (see below) is common on
Astove and Cosmoledo. Even on Assumption the sunbird has
survived the guano exploitation which has caused the extinction
of three other species of land bird. The diet of this species is
partly nectar and partly insects: it has been found to eat caterpillars, beetles, and even ants, as well as small spiders, and it is
often seen probing flowers with its specially adapted bill.

The nest is a domed structure about the size and shape of a
small coconut, suspended at the top from a slender branch,
usually about two metres from the ground. Nests are not uncommonly found below ground level, however, suspended inside
sink holes in the weathered coral, and from time to time even
inside buildings. The entrance to the nest is in the side, and
there is often a 'porch' over it. The female builds alone, and she

also has most if not all of the responsibility of incubation, in common with the sunbirds of southern Africa. The season is long, at least from August to March. The clutch is two eggs, ivory with dark reddish speckles, very small. The male takes some part in feeding the young, but irregularly compared with the diligent female. The eggs hatch in thirteen days, and the young birds take less than three weeks to fledge, when they have the dull plumage of the female.

Sunbirds in the Aldabra group, like those in Seychelles (page 106), seem to have suffered little if at all from the arrival of man, even on poor blasted Assumption. They can have few enemies; their nests are inaccessible to rats and lizards, and their diet, with its insectivorous content and evident adaptability to introduced flowering plants, is readily supplied. Sunbirds have been seen mobbing coucals more than once, which might indicate some predation, but apart from this they seem to be without enemies.

Sunbirds are mainly an African group, though there are numerous species to the east, as far as Australia; and there is even one as far north as Palestine. Many of the African sunbirds in particular are very brightly coloured – they have names like the Superb Sunbird, the Splendid Sunbird, and the Scarlet-tufted Malachite Sunbird – but among the islands they tend to be drab. The series in the Aldabra group is descended from the Malagasy species, *Nectarinia sovimanga*: at Aldabra *N. s. aldabrensis* is distinct from *N. s. abbotti*, only twenty miles away on Assumption, and both are distinct from *N. s. buchenorum*, of Cosmoledo and Astove. The differences are primarily concerned with the colour of the underparts, but for field purposes the distribution is distinction enough. The birds are separated within such a small area, after all, because they do not normally fly from one island to another. There is a highly distinct species in central Seychelles, which is considered next.

SEYCHELLES SUNBIRD Colibri *Nectarinia dussumieri*
Sey   **Pl. 7**

By comparison with African sunbirds the Seychelles species is
drab, duller even than the Aldabra birds, and because of its
more insular situation it is also larger. The male in breeding
dress has a deep metallic blue breast, and bright orange or
yellow pectoral tufts; the female is dull grey below and dark
above. As at Aldabra, the male has a complex trilling song,
perhaps more repetitive than the Souimanga Sunbird, but no
less vehement. The female does not sing, but both sexes have
similar flight and alarm calls to the Aldabra birds.

Sunbirds are to be seen everywhere in Seychelles, more commonly
in the hills in forested places, but also on the plateau, especially
on La Digue. The diet is chiefly nectar with a large insect
component, especially during the breeding season.

In Seychelles, sunbirds breed from October through to March
in large numbers, but there are a few nests to be found at all
times of the year. The curved beak of the incubating female
identifies an active nest. The nest is typical, coconut shaped,
hanging on longer strands than at Aldabra, perhaps because it is
usually in a more sheltered site in woodland. It may be quite
high up, sometimes as much as forty feet, often in a *Casuarina*
tree. The porched entrance leads to a spherical nesting chamber
lined with kapok, cotton wool, and small feathers. Any suitable
material is used for the outer structure, including of course grass
and *Casuarina* needles, but also spider's web, and pieces of string
and domestic debris. The male is said to lay the first foundation,
but thereafter the female does all the building. She seems to
court a sticky death as she hovers in front of spider's webs
collecting strands with which to bind the nest. The clutch is one
egg, not two as is normal at Aldabra, but the egg looks the same.
Parent birds have been seen collecting insects from spider's webs
to feed the chick.

Like the bulbul, and the other sunbirds, the Seychelles Sunbird
seems to have adapted well to the presence of man. It nests and
feeds successfully on introduced plants which its ancestors never

saw, such as *Hibiscus* and *Canna* lilies; and the design and siting of the nest keeps the bird safe from predators such as rats and cats.

The origins of the Seychelles species are thought to be Malagasy or African, but as Benson has pointed out, it has diverged so far from the parent stock that it is impossible to be sure where it came from. The range of sunbirds is beautifully illustrated in G. E. Shelley's *Monograph of the Nectariniidae* (1876–80), a rare book, but one worth looking out in good museums if you are interested in the variation within this single family of small birds. The sunbirds of the Indian Ocean are described by C. W. Benson in *Animals*, vol. 12, p. 497, together with illustrations of them all by Chloë Talbot Kelly.

MADAGASCAR WHITE-EYE Oiseau lunette
Zosterops maderaspatana subspp.   **Pl. 7**
Ald Cos—Ast

The white-eye is a very small leaf-green bird with pale under-parts, very well camouflaged, with a clear white ring round the eye, and a short bill. There is no visible difference between the sexes. The voice is a sweet 'wee-eet' or 'chee-r' call, rather like a tiny silver bell, repeated by members of a flock.

White-eyes are only slightly less numerous than sunbirds on Aldabra, but on Cosmoledo and Astove they are much less common, and they are absent altogether from Assumption. Their favoured habitat is among thickets in open scrub, but they are seen in all types of vegetation including mangroves. They tend to move in flocks of between eight and thirty birds, with continuous calling. Their diet includes insects such as bugs, weevils, and grubs from buds, and also the eggs and adults of ants. In southern Africa some white-eyes eat nectar, piercing the bases of flowers with their bills before removing the nectar with their brush tongues, but although the Aldabra White-eye has a similar tongue it has never been seen to feed in this way.

The breeding of the species is not well known. The season is apparently from September to March, that is, during the wetter part of the year. The nest is a small neat open cup, bound on to fine branches about two or three metres up in a bush. The only clutch ever found, by Abbott in 1895, consisted of two small pale green eggs. Courtship, observed in November, consists of mutual preening round the head and especially the eye-ring, with the birds very close together, practically leaning on each other. A variety of different calls is heard at this time, including a harsh trilled version of the 'wee-eet', and a ringing 'tweet' song from one of the birds.

White-eyes, like sunbirds, seem to have escaped the worst effects of man's arrival. Although they probably suffer some predation from the kestrel, this can be only slight, and they have a wide and easily supplied diet: thus they are relatively safe from disturbance by man. There has never been a record of a white-eye from Assumption, and perhaps they never occurred there; they would have been hard to miss. There may be some competition with the sunbird on the islands where the two coexist, since they have very similar diets, but there is no evidence that the white-eye is in decline.

White-eyes are very widespread all over the world, on tropical islands especially. They are among the most successful invaders and colonisers, perhaps because they move in flocks, so that if one managed to invade an island it would most probably not be alone. There are forty-nine species of white-eyes east of Pakistan, and only four in Africa, though those four have many subspecies. There are nine species on the islands to the east and west of Africa. The subspecies on Aldabra is unique, known as Z. m. aldabrensis; the white-eyes on Astove are indistinguishable from nominate maderaspatana of Madagascar; and although it has been suggested that the birds on Cosmoledo might constitute a separate subspecies, menaiensis, this is not yet certain.

The surviving white-eye in Seychelles is not closely related, and was once included in a different genus.

SEYCHELLES (GREY) WHITE-EYE   Oiseau banane
Zosterops modesta   **Pl. 7**
Sey

The Seychelles White-eye is smaller than a sunbird, dull grey-brown in colour, with the typical clear ring of white feathers round the eye. The underparts are paler grey, like those of a female sunbird, but the bill is short and straight. The voice is very like the flock call of the Aldabra species, but more trilled.

The distribution of the white-eye is restricted now, whatever it may have been in the past; it is to be seen in the high forest, on Mahé only, in places like Souvenir, Morne Blanc, Forêt Noire, and occasionally at La Misère, in the clove trees. Its diet is not known, but it is presumably similar to that of the Aldabra bird, that is insects collected round flowers, with perhaps a little nectar.

The nest of the species has never been seen, and nothing is known about its breeding behaviour. It seems reasonable to assume that the nest will not be markedly different from that found on Aldabra, a small tidy cup built among slender twigs, possibly high up in a tree. This is one of the places in Seychelles ornithology where any observer might be the first to find the information; when you take a walk in the forest, keep a look out for a small fallen basket-nest, and bring it down with you to the Department of Agriculture, together with a record of its location, what kind of tree it was near, and any other information you can. Of course, one must never touch or otherwise disturb an active nest, but any information will be new to science.

There were once two white-eyes in Seychelles: *Z. mayottensis* on Marianne, and *Z. modesta* on Mahé. Neither has ever been recorded from another island. This, the survivor, was thought to be extinct from 1936 until it was rediscovered by Philippe Lalanne in 1962. For a long time it was included in the separate genus, *Malacirops*, together with the other grey rather than green white-eye of the area, the species *borbonica* of Mauritius and Réunion. Both these species show marked insular characteristics, and both may have shared a remote ancestor in Africa rather than Asia.

The extinct Chestnut-flanked White-eye of Seychelles, now known to science as *Zosterops mayottensis semiflava*, was another example, with the Black Parrot and especially the bulbul, of the close avifaunal link between Seychelles and the Comoros, to the north-west of Madagascar. Its only relative in the same species is *Z. m. mayottensis*, of Mayotte in Comoros. Another Madagascar species of white-eye, *Z. maderaspatana*, has spread to the islands of the Aldabra group as well as the Comoros, but *Z. mayottensis* seems to have evolved as a species in the Comoros, whence it must have reached Seychelles without succeeding in colonising Madagascar on the way. Some authors can find no difference between skins of the two 'subspecies' from Seychelles and the Comoros. It has recently become possible to sort out these matters by means of behavioural and ecological separations, but unfortunately the material to work on no longer exists. This is a very strong reason for the continued protection of the surviving white-eye, whose taxonomic position and distributional history are also in doubt.

HOUSE SPARROW Moineau *Passer domesticus indicus*
Ami ??*Sey* **Pl. 8**

A very familiar bird, yet unexpected in the Amirantes, the House Sparrow in these parts is somewhat smaller and brighter coloured than the common sparrow in Europe, though its general appearance is the same. Males in breeding have a conspicuous black bib. The voice is very similar, too, a chirping sound which becomes more resonant and penetrating in breeding males.

The House Sparrow was introduced from India to South-east Africa, Zanzibar, and the Comoros some long time ago, and it is well established there: presumably it was introduced into the Amirantes from Africa, probably by accident in a shipload of rice. It occurs and breeds on Desroches, Resource, St Joseph, D'Arros, and Alphonse – and probably other islands in the Amirantes. I saw a flock of about twenty sparrows behind the Post Office in Victoria in 1965, but only once, and nowhere else in central Seychelles. There is no record of sparrows in Seychelles before or since, so perhaps they were new arrivals which failed to establish a colony.

House Sparrows are omnivorous, and commensal with man, but their chicks are fed on insects while they are in the nest, and for about the first fortnight after they fledge.

The nest of the House Sparrow is a vast untidy bundle of grassy material and feathers, commonly in or a building. The clutch over the range as a whole varies from two to seven eggs, but the season's production of chicks is greatly increased by the frequency of nesting: in India, pairs of sparrows produce between three and six broods per season, depending on the weather. There is no information on their breeding frequency in the Amirantes, but it is probably similar. The breeding season of the species is more or less continuous, with individual pairs coming into season at all times of year. The survival of the large numbers of young which are hatched depends on the supply of insects available to each brood; there is a very high infant mortality. This makes the House Sparrow very hard to control, since killing some birds merely makes life easier for the others, and chicks which would have died in the natural way are given a new chance to survive. If the sparrow succeeds eventually in colonising Seychelles, it will be very hard to eradicate. If in fact there have been unsuccessful pioneer groups from time to time which have failed, it might be through competition with the ubiquitous Madagascar Fody.

RED-HEADED FOREST FODY   Cardinal (♂); Serin (♀)
Foudia eminentissima aldabrana   **Pl. 8**
Ald

The male cardinal in breeding dress is unmistakable, with scarlet head and breast, yellow belly, and orange-red rump. The streaky brown wings may be suffused with red at the height of

Plate 7   SUNBIRDS AND WHITE-EYES

1. **Souimanga Sunbird** *Nectarinia sovimanga*   p. 104
   Small active bird with sharply decurved bill, dark in colour.
   a, Male *N.s. aldabrensis*: in breeding dress has metallic green
   head and mantle, red and black breast bands, yellow axillary
   tufts.
   b, Female *N.s. aldabrensis*: drab and streaky with lightly
   barred throat. Juveniles and non-breeding males similar.
   c, Male *N.s. abbotti*: rather as *aldabrensis*, but both sexes at
   all ages have dark underparts. Assumption only.

2. **Seychelles Sunbird** *Nectarinia dussumieri*   p. 106
   Dark-coloured Sunbird, similar in habits and appearance to
   Souimanga.
   a, Male: breeding dress has metallic blue throat, and yellow
   or orange axillary tufts (colour varies).
   b. Female: very drab, paler below.

3. **Seychelles (Grey) White-eye** *Zosterops modesta*   p. 109
   Small dingy bird, inconspicuous. Rare, known only from
   mountains of Mahé.

4. **Madagascar White-eye** *Zosterops maderaspatana*   p. 107
   Very small active leaf-green bird, usually moves in flocks.

1. **Red-headed Forest Fody** *Foudia eminentissima aldabrana* p. 111
Sparrow sized weaver. Common Aldabra.
a, Male: breeding dress. Head and breast red-orange. Bill black.
b, Female: dull yellowish, rather streaky. Bill horn colour.
Non-breeding males similar to females.

2. **Madagascar Fody** *Foudia madagascariensis* p. 115
Distinguished from Seychelles Fody by smaller size, lighter colour, and shorter bill, when not in breeding dress.
a, Breeding male: bright red all over head and underparts, streaked with brown on wings. Rare flavistic variant has yellow replacing red.
b, Female and juvenile: brown and streaky on back, paler below.

3. **Seychelles Fody** *Foudia sechellarum* p. 117
Cousin, Cousine and Frigate only. Larger than **2,** darker brown, and has longer, slightly decurved bill.
a, Breeding male: golden throat and forehead.
b, Female and juvenile: very drab-coloured; somewhat paler below.

4. **House Sparrow** *Passer domesticus indicus* p. 110
As English Sparrow, but slightly smaller and brighter coloured. Breeding males (illustrated) have black bib. Non-breeders and females distinguished from Madagascar Fody by more chestnut colour.

5. **Common Waxbill** *Estrilda astrild* p. 119
Very small, dark brown, finch-like bird. Red bill and head patch, red stripe down breast.

6. **Mozambique Serin** *Serinus mozambicus* p. 120
Small, canary-yellow finch with brown streaky back. May still occur in Amirantes.
B.S.

H

breeding condition. Females and non-breeding birds are dull greenish-brown, and streaky. All have heavy triangular bills, black in breeding males. The voice is a high-pitched 'tweet'; the male has a wide variety of songs based on this and on fizzing sounds and a peculiar 'bottle-filling' song, heard near the nest during breeding.

The fody is widespread over most of Aldabra, though it is not common among the dunes of the south coast. Elsewhere it is very numerous and conspicuous, especially among mangroves and *Casuarina* groves. It lives happily in commensalism with man round the houses at the settlement, becoming quite tame. It has a large bill for its kind, seemingly an adaptation to a wide range of food sizes; but although it will eat anything round the house, in the wild its diet proves to be surprisingly insectivorous, with few records of plant foods being taken. This is similar to another insular fody, the Toq Toq of Seychelles, which is also more insectivorous than might perhaps be expected; it is an example of the occupation of an unadopted niche in the open island ecological situation.

The fody breeds at Aldabra from November through to March or even April. The nest is a football-shaped object, built of grass roots and lined with finer material, usually about four or five metres up in cover, quite commonly mangroves or dense *Pemphis* scrub, and also in *Casuarina* trees. The outside of the nest may be decorated with leaves of *Casuarina*, or other plant material. Artificial nesting material is often collected round houses, including the straws from brooms, and cotton wool. Males do most of the building of the nest, and females seem to take responsibility for incubation. While the male is building, it exhibits a territorial display pattern in which the feathers of the rump are raised, and the tail and wings lowered, accompanied by fizzing and tweeting calls. The clutch is two or three pale blue eggs, clear and glossy.

The distribution of the cardinal seems to be unaffected by the presence of man, and it has no serious predators. A point worth stressing, however, is that although as yet the Madagascar Fody,

F. madagascariensis, does not occur on Aldabra, if it were to be introduced, as it has been on to so many other islands in the area, it would quite possibly have an adverse effect on the Aldabra birds through competition.

Foudia eminentissima is represented also in the Comoros and Madagascar, but which of those populations gave rise to the Aldabra subspecies is not known. R. E. Moreau, who made a detailed study of the genus, was of the opinion that the species could have evolved in Comoros from African stock, and colonised Madagascar and Aldabra from there, but I can see no way in which this could be clarified, although it would throw some interesting light on the possible origins of some of the other birds of Aldabra if it were. The Aldabra Fody is not known from any of the other islands in the group, though it may well have occurred at least on Assumption in the past.

MADAGASCAR FODY Cardinal *Foudia madagascariensis*
Sey Ami   **Pl. 8**

The only other bird in Seychelles with which the small finch-like cardinal is likely to be confused is the Seychelles Fody, *F. sechellarum*, but since the latter occurs only on three small islands, while the Madagascar species is widespread on all, such confusion will be rare. The male cardinal is not likely to be confused with anything else (except perhaps a particularly bright red flower); but the female in her dowdy brown dress, or the non-breeding male in his, are rather undistinguished. The principal difference is in size and general colour: the Madagascar bird is smaller and more slightly built, and its colour is more yellowish brown and streaky, while the Seychelles species is darker brown and much more sturdily built (see page 117). The voice of the cardinal has been described as being more like an insect than a bird – a very high-pitched 'tseee', or a brisk chirrup. The territorial song of the male is also very high, bubbling and hissing like a tiny steam engine.

The cardinal is very common in the lowlands of all the islands in the granitic group, especially round habitation, for it is strongly commensal. The species has been introduced into most of the Amirante Islands, and it is common on Farquhar. Its diet is principally seeds, except in the breeding season, when it takes mostly insects to feed its young. At this time there might be some competition between the introduced cardinal and the endemic species, but the latter with its much more wide-ranging diet seems to be in no danger from this.

The nest of the cardinal is a domed structure like that of the other fodies in this book, smaller and more delicate than that of the Seychelles Fody, and often built in a coconut palm rather than lower down in bushes. The eggs are pale blue and very glossy, usually two or three in number, though as many as five have been recorded. The breeding season is during the north-west monsoon, from November to about March or April, but before this the males may be seen in full breeding dress forming flocks of up to thirty birds together, a spectacular sight. The display of the male is similar to that already described for the Aldabra bird.

The cardinal seems to have been introduced into Seychelles in about 1860 or perhaps earlier; the story attached to the event is probably not true, though it is rather fun. It seems that there were two neighbours who were in dispute over the ownership of a plot of land where one of them was growing rice. The frustrated party, to gain revenge on his rival, sent to Mauritius for some cardinals, which were known to be a plague of ricefields, and released them into his neighbour's territory. From that day to this, it has been well-nigh impossible to grow rice in Mahé. Even if it is more likely that the cardinal was introduced as a cage bird, it's a nice tale. From Seychelles proper the cardinal was introduced to most of the cultivated Amirantes, possibly in some cases by accident, and there it flourishes. It is absent from Alphonse, however.

There is a popular belief that the cardinal drove the native species out of the larger islands; but in this respect it is worth noting that when Newton visited Seychelles in 1865 he found only the cardinal on Mahé, despite searching for some finch-like bird from the native avifauna. Cardinals arrived on Praslin before 1904, on Cousin after 1940, and on Cousine not until 1958, but they are now common on all the islands.

In its native Madagascar the cardinal is a savannah species, frequenting open grassland and leaving the forest to specialists such as *F. eminentissima*. It could never have survived in old Seychelles before man cut down the trees; but by the time it was introduced the open plantations provided it with just the niche it required, and with its fearless commensalism it was bound to succeed. It seems to have done no harm, and it is certainly an attractive garden bird, sufficiently so to enable men to forgive it its share of their crops.

SEYCHELLES FODY Toq Toq *Foudia sechellarum* Pl. 8
Sey (?Ami)

The Toq Toq, the truly Seychellois weaver, is a sturdy dark-brown bird with a rather long slightly curved beak. The male in breeding dress assumes a golden crown and bib, and develops a black bill, but is otherwise drab in the extreme compared with the other fodies in the area. The best distinction from the cardinal on the three islands where they coexist is that the Toq Toq is larger and more evenly coloured, lacking the streaky wings and back of the smaller bird. The voice of the Toq Toq is what gives it its Créole name; feeding parties give a 'tsk tsk' call continually, presumably as a means of social contact. The alarm call is an angry chatter, which may be taken up in concert by other birds nearby: while they are breeding the males sing, a version of the territorial song which they use to warn other birds off an egg which they are eating – a series of piercing 'tweet' calls.

Toq Toqs are found only on Cousin, Cousine, and Frigate in the central group. A few were introduced to D'Arros in the Amirantes in 1965 by the Bristol Seychelles Expedition, but we have not heard of them since 1968, when they were still surviving. On the islands where they occur, the birds are more common in the plateau and less so in the hills. Their diet is catholic, including insects, fruit, and copra, as well as seeds. They also have a taste for the eggs of sea birds, particularly Fairy Terns and Lesser Noddies, when the parents are disturbed; the Toq Toqs show a high degree of specialisation in this predation, having techniques for dealing not only with the egg, but with the lizards which flock to the spot where the egg hits the ground when it is knocked off its perch. From my observations, some Toq Toqs are habitual egg-thieves, while others, which live in places where other foods are more easily obtainable, hardly ever take eggs. Nevertheless, in the seabird colonies predation by Toq Toqs must be a considerable factor in limiting the size of the season's crop of chicks.

Toq Toqs breed all the year round, with a peak in September and October, at the end of the south-east monsoon. The nest is a large and rather untidy structure, spherical as in the other fodies, built rather low down in bushes as a rule, but occasionally in coconut palms and tall *Casuarina* trees. The parents co-operate in building and incubation, and later in feeding the chicks. The clutch is two or three white eggs, but it seems as if only one of the brood survives to fledge – at any rate all the family parties I have seen contained only one young bird.

The first collected specimen of the Toq Toq came from Marianne, where it is now extinct. When Newton collected it in 1865, he was told that the species was still to be seen, if rarely, on La Digue. There are five skins in museums in England labelled simply 'Praslin', but it is not certain quite where they came from; perhaps Cousin or Cousine, regarded as off-islands of Praslin. The species seems never to have been known on Mahé or Silhouette. Why the Toq Toq died out on the other islands is not known, but the study of its ecology by John Hurrell Crook indicated that competition with the introduced cardinal was probably not the cause.

The Toq Toq is typically insular in its drab colour, its large size, and its longer bill and consequently more varied diet than other fodies. It is related to the Madagascar fodies, though it differs from them in having yellow rather than red as the breeding colour. The yellow species on Rodriguez, *F. flavicans*, may be closely related (cf. *Bebrornis rodericana*): it is one of the only two surviving endemic species on that island, and the latest intelligence is that it is outnumbered by about ten to one by the introduced species, *F. madagascariensis*.

The Toq Toq is another of the rare endemic species which is protected by the sanctuary established on Cousin Island by the International Council for Bird Preservation.

COMMON WAXBILL Bengali *Estrilda astrild* Pl. 8
Sey Ami

Commonly seen in flocks, waxbills are small dark-brown finch-like birds with bright red bill and head patch, and a red streak down the breast. Their voice is a subdued sparrow-like chatter.

Waxbills are seen on La Digue, where the grassland begins to take over from the swamp, and down the west coast of Mahé, where there are similar wettish grassy places. They are seed-eaters, feeding on grass-heads and among other seeding herbs. The size of the feeding party, about twenty or thirty birds together as a rule, seems to make the birds very alert, and as a flock they are shy. A whole flock will flicker and fly away as one bird if it is not approached with care and delicacy.

The waxbill breeds during the north-west monsoon, from about October to March; the nest is an untidy handful of grass stems built into the fork of a low bush. It is domed, with a straight tunnel entrance. I have no accurate figure for the clutch size: the southern African population lays usually from four to six tiny white eggs, and Lalanne (1963) gives the same figure for the Seychelles birds.

The waxbill is the first introduced bird to be mentioned in Seychelles, in the manuscript account by de Malavois, quoted at the beginning of this book. In his account he says it is among the most numerous birds of Mahé, along with a parakeet. (The parakeet must have been the Seychelles Green, now extinct.) Both these species, according to de Malavois, did great harm to the crops of the settlers, which gives us a clue to the cause of extinction of the parakeet. At present the waxbill is less numerous than in de Malavois' description, probably not so much because it has been reduced by persecution, but because fewer seed crops are grown, and most of the wet grasslands which the species prefers have been drained and used as plantations.

The waxbill was surely brought in from Africa as a cage-bird, probably by the ladies among the earliest settlers. Some people suggest that they are in fact natural colonists; but had they been, they might be expected to have diverged in size or appearance from their African relatives. In fact they are absolutely identical, which suggests a recent arrival.

Waxbills are found on Alphonse, and were once recorded on Desroches, in the Amirantes, where they were presumably introduced in the same way as into Seychelles.

MOZAMBIQUE SERIN   Serin   *Serinus mozambicus*   Pl. 8
?Ami

The serin was introduced into the Amirantes very early in their history – it was collected on Desroches by Coppinger in 1884 and again by Abbott in 1892 – but it has become very rare since then, and may have died out. It is a small canary finch, yellow-breasted, darker and streaky above, which moves in flocks high in *Casuarina* trees. It is a seed-eater, but Coppinger's report that he saw them commonly in coconut palms may indicate that they eat (ate?) the male flowers, as do fodies in Seychelles.

There is no information on the nesting of serins in the Amirantes: in other places the nest is a small sturdy cup, built by the female alone. The clutch is four to six eggs, blue more or less streaked with red. The young are fed by regurgitation of seeds collected by the female.

The serin has failed to emulate the success of other cage-bird escapes in these islands, probably because its ecological niche, like that of the waxbill to some extent, was too close to that of the successful fodies. The hearsay record of a 'serin' on Cosmoledo at the turn of the century may well be based on an error of understanding: the female Forest Fody is often called 'serin' by the Seychellois.

WEDGE-TAILED SHEARWATER Fouquet
Puffinus pacificus chlororhynchus　　　　　　　　　　**Pl. 9**
Ami Sey

A large heavily built brown-grey bird, darker on wings and tail, the Wedge-tailed Shearwater is commonly seen in the evenings and early mornings round its breeding islands at the right time of year. The flight of shearwaters is distinctive, wheeling low over the water with stiff wings. The tail of this species is distinctly wedge-shaped when it is slightly spread, distinguishing it from the rare Flesh-footed Shearwater, *Puffinus carneipes*, which has a shorter rounded tail. The feet of the wedge-tail vary in colour from black to pink, but the outer toe and web, and the outside of the leg, are dark even in individuals with paler feet. From May to September paler abrasion lines are visible on the otherwise dark grey wings. The species is silent in the air, but on its breeding islands it utters all night an unmistakable series of wails, screams, and hooting calls when it is on the ground.

The Wedge-tailed Shearwater breeds in Seychelles, on the rat-free islands, especially Cousin, Cousine, and Aride, in large dense colonies; also on Desnoeufs and Desroches, and probably other islands, in the Amirantes. Nest-selection and burrowing take place in June–October, egg-laying in November, incubation and fledging December–March; and during these periods the birds are to be seen coming in to land on the islands at dusk, and leaving very early in the morning. 'Rafts' of as many as a thousand birds together may be seen on the surface of the sea, often out of sight of land, but regularly near the breeding islands. Shearwaters feed sitting on the surface, well away from land, taking flying fish and squid.

The nests are burrows in the rocky hillsides in the granitic islands, or in sandy soil on the coral islands. The burrows may be up to six feet long, or among rocks even longer where the surface permits; on the other hand, I have found birds on eggs under tufts of grass on Cousin, where the rocky surface prohibits any burrowing at all in some places. The single large white egg is incubated by both parents in turn, in shifts of about a week each, for sixty to seventy days; the grey downy chick is incubated for about a week, and then left while the parents go to seek food. Thereafter the chick is fed at irregular intervals which may be as long as ten days; it is able to survive this regime because it can lay down large deposits of fat – at the peak of its growth it can weigh twice as much as the parents, reaching 500 grammes. The chicks are not fed for the last ten days of their 90–100 day fledging period, and during this time they lose weight steadily until they reach flying weight. It is said that after they have left their native island they may not make a landfall again for three or four years, when they return to the same island to breed; but this is not yet proved.

The numbers of Wedge-tailed Shearwater in Seychelles have been severely depleted by the cropping of chicks for food, but now that this practice has stopped on most of the Fouquet islands the populations are recovering. The colony on Cousin numbered nearly 10,000 pairs in 1970, and that on Aride is surely larger. The only natural enemy of the species on its breeding ground is the endemic egg-eating skink, *Mabuya wrightii*, which accounted for nearly ten per cent of eggs laid on Cousin in 1970. Rats, introduced by man, have driven the shearwater out of its breeding sites on the larger islands.

AUDUBON'S (DUSKY) SHEARWATER Riga
Puffinus lherminieri nicolae   **Pl. 9**
Ald   Cos   Ast   ?*Ami*   Sey

Audubon's (sometimes called the Dusky) Shearwater is much smaller than the wedge-tailed, black above and white below. It flies in the same style over the sea, but over land it has a hovering way of flying, with short quick wing-beats. It calls in the air at this time, a hair-raising scream followed by a gurgling sound. Again unlike the wedge-tailed, it is silent on the ground for most of the night, calling again when it leaves the island in the morning. It comes to land in full darkness, usually after seven o'clock in the evening, and leaves well before dawn.

Audubon's Shearwater breeds in Seychelles on Cousin, Cousine, and probably also Aride; it is known to breed on Aldabra, Astove, and Cosmoledo, and probably also Desnoeufs. It is not colonial in the same way as the wedge-tailed, making its narrow burrows often round the edge of a wedge-tailed colony. Since the smaller species needs much smaller holes, there is not much competition between the two for nesting places, but in at least one instance an Audubon's drove a wedge-tailed from a burrow where the larger bird already had an egg. Audubon's Shearwater has no defined non-breeding season, so it may be seen round the breeding islands at most times of year. It feeds on flying fish and squid, taken from the surface, in the same way as the wedge-tailed.

The nesting burrows are typically just too small to get the hand into, and often very long; a single white egg is laid, incubated by both parents in turn for two or three days at a time. The incubation period is forty-two to fifty days, and fledging takes about seventy-five days, the chick being fed every other night. The peak weight of the chicks on Cousin in 1970 averaged 250 grammes, compared with the adult weight of 160 to 200 grammes. The starvation period before the chick flies may be as short as three days, but is usually about seven.

Audubon's Shearwater seems to suffer less from predation by skinks than the wedge-tailed, perhaps because its narrower burrows are more easily defended.

Individuals are often picked up on liners at night, flying into the lights when they are disturbed from roosting on the water. They should be handled in a cloth, to avoid damaging the feathers, and placed in a safe dark place until they fly away – but look out for rings first, and record the number!

STORM PETRELS Satanic Various species   **Pl. 9**
Seen at sea. No local breeding place known

Storm Petrels are small, dark, long-legged birds, seen fluttering
close to the surface of the sea, usually out of sight of land. They
often follow ships, feeding in the wake, their legs dangling and
sometimes pattering on the surface – hence the derivation of the
name from that of St Peter. Identification is not easy: there are
three main groups represented in these waters.

Dark with white rump
Oceanites oceanicus Wilson's Storm Petrel Breeds in southern
ocean in December, migrates north March–April, south again in
November. Recorded in Seychelles in November. Pale band on
upper wing, *yellow* webs to feet.
Hydrobates pelagicus British Storm Petrel Breeds Europe and
Mediterranean, winters south to Red Sea; possible near Seychelles. Appearance as Wilson's but has pale patch *below* base of
wing, black feet.

Dark all over (not illustrated)
Oceanodroma monorhis Swinhoe's Storm Petrel A north Pacific
species, but migrates very widely and may well occur in western
Indian Ocean. General colour in good light is *brown* not black.
O. matsudairae Black Storm Petrel Japanese breeder, also
highly migratory, not unlikely in these waters, some records,
mostly to north of Seychelles. General colour *black* in good light,
paler on upper wing coverts.

White underparts
Pelagodroma marina White-faced Storm Petrel Unlikely in
Seychelles, rare west of 80° E. Underparts, face, line above eye,
white; dark above, upper tail paler.
Fregetta tropica Black-bellied Storm Petrel White below, black
stripe along belly; white rump, otherwise dark above with paler
wing bar. Some records in nearby waters, just possible.

As can be seen from these notes, the distribution of Storm Petrels is not known with any certainty. Any sighting should be reported, accompanied with details of location and date, and a description of the bird in as much detail as possible.

WHITE-TAILED TROPICBIRD   Paille en Queue
Phaëthon lepturus lepturus   **Pl. 10**
Ald Sey ?Ami

A large heavily built white bird with black markings on wings and head, yellow bill; adults have two long white tail streamers which project a foot or more beyond the rest of the tail. Juveniles are barred silver and black, looking grey in flight, and they lack the streamers. The voice in the air is a curious 'sneezing' sound given by birds performing the stiff-winged courtship flight. On the nest a variety of screams and squawks is given.

White-tailed Tropicbirds breed throughout the year: on islets in the lagoon at Aldabra; probably also on some islands in the Amirantes, though there are no confirmed reports; and commonly on small islands in Seychelles, as well as high in the mountain forests of the large islands. They feed out to sea as a rule, diving for their food, often from a considerable height. Their diet is flying fish and squid, in common with most of the other large seabirds of these waters.

The nest of the tropicbird is either on the ground, beneath a bush or a rock, or in the buttress of large trees; or in the forest, high up in a large tree or a crevice in the rock face. One egg is laid, ivory with dark crimson spots, the spots sometimes so close together as to give the egg the colour of mahogany. The incubation period is five weeks, during which both parents take turns of a day or more; both also feed the chick during the eight-week fledging period. The chick reaches a peak weight of more than 500 grammes, twice that of the parents, before losing weight rapidly during the last week of fledging. The bill of the white-tailed chick is grey, not black like that of the Red-tailed Tropicbird. The parents 'sit tight' when discovered on the nest, and will defend themselves fiercely with their sharp bills – you have been warned.

Tropicbirds have been cropped in the past for food, in the same way as shearwaters; on the Fouquet islands their nests are often among the shearwater colony. I am told that in Bermuda the same species breeds on islands infested with rats, but in Seychelles and at Aldabra rats and tropicbirds do not coexist.

Breeding adults in Seychelles have a beautiful apricot-coloured flush to the feathers of breast and neck.

RED-TAILED TROPICBIRD Quelec *Phaethon*
rubricauda rubricauda   **Pl. 10**
Cos Ald ??Sey

Very similar in size and in its rapid-beating flight to the white-tailed, the Red-tailed Tropicbird has much less black on the wings, and its tail streamers are red (and much less conspicuous in flight). The bill, too, is bright red.

The Red-tailed Tropicbird is a great rarity in central Seychelles, though it is said that one or two pairs still breed on Aride, where they used to be common. The last definite record of them was in 1968, when the owner reported that two or three young of this species (distinguished by their black bills) had been killed and eaten by his staff. However, at Aldabra and Cosmoledo the species is common, breeding on islets in the lagoon in much the same sites as the white-tailed, and it is often seen at sea around the islands.

As with the white-tailed, there is no marked breeding season for Red-tailed Tropicbirds. The way of life of the two species is in fact closely similar, the only distinctions being small matters: for example, at Aldabra the red-tailed nests more often on the surface, and the white-tailed more often in solution holes in the rock; the red-tailed eats more fish and of a larger size than the white-tailed, which takes relatively more squid. The ecological separation between the two species is not yet worked out.

The Red-tailed Tropicbird has a pink flush in breeding adults, not apricot as in the other species; on the nest the adult looks as if it is glowing from within. Both species are equally fierce in defending their nest and young.

RED-FOOTED BOOBY Fou bête *Sula sula rubripes* **Pl. 10**
Ald Cos Far (ex *Ass Ast*) (*Sey*)

Boobies are large powerfully built gannets, with heavy bills and a bald area round the eye which gives them their peculiarly vacuous expression, and presumably their uncomplimentary name. The Red-footed Booby is white, with black wing-*tips* and very conspicuous rubbery red feet. Juveniles are chocolate-brown all over, again with bright red feet. Some adults are 'brown-phase' birds, dull brown all over except for white tail and lower belly. The adults have a harsh and very loud 'arrival call' when they return to the nest, but otherwise they are silent in the air.

The Red-footed Booby breeds at Aldabra, Cosmoledo, and Farquhar, mostly from November to March, but in certain colonies at other times of the year. In the morning and evening large numbers may be seen flying out to sea from the breeding colonies, or returning with food. At this time they are much persecuted by Frigate Birds, which chase them to steal their crop contents, regurgitated by the booby in the course of trying to escape. The diet of the booby, obtained by diving, is the inevitable flying fish and squid.

The nests are built in mangroves, and both parents share the incubation of the single large white egg. The downy chick is very readily tamed, and on the outer islands many fishermen have one as a pet. The booby is astonishingly tame on the nest: it can even be lifted off an egg, its ring number recorded, and replaced, without so much as a struggle. This may be in response to living in close proximity with the piratical frigates, which will remove the nest stick by stick as soon as it is vacated.

Juvenile Red-footed Boobies range widely after fledging, and they are sometimes seen in central Seychelles in September and October, along with a few vagrant adults.

Plate 9   SHEARWATERS AND STORM PETRELS

1. **Audubon's (Dusky) Shearwater**   *Puffinus*   p. 122
   lherminieri nicolae
   Much smaller than **2**, white below. Swifter flight, approaches
   land later in evening. Chicks: in burrows year round but
   rare; grey not black.

2. **Wedge-tailed Shearwater**   *Puffinus pacificus chlororhyncus*   p. 121
   Large dark-coloured bird, wheels low over water on stiff
   wings. Common around smaller granitic islands, Central
   Group and some Amirantes, late in evening. Chicks: black
   and downy, in burrows December-March. Surface feeder,
   out of sight of land.

3. **White-faced Storm Petrel**   *Pelagodroma marina*   p. 124
   Small, dark, long-legged bird (as are all Storm Petrels)
   flying close to surface of water, feet dangling. Larger than
   Wilson's and British; dark above, white below, conspicuous
   white stripe above eye giving very pale appearance.

4. **British Storm Petrel**   *Hydrobates pelagicus*   p. 124
   Much as Wilson's and difficult to distinguish. Pale below
   wing, feet black.

5. **Wilson's Storm Petrel**   *Oceanites oceanicus*   p. 124
   White rump, otherwise dark all over; yellow webs to feet.

6. **Black-bellied Storm Petrel**   *Fregetta tropica*   p. 124
   Dark above with white rump, pale wing-bar; white below
   with black stripe along belly.

FRIGATEBIRDS, TROPICBIRDS AND BOOBIES

Plate 10

1. Lesser Frigate *Fregata ariel* p. 131
Shape overhead unmistakeable as a Frigate: long angled wings, black with or without white markings, hangs motionless on the wind.
a, Adult male: white patches at base of wings.
b, Adult female: white patch of variable shape and size.

2. Great Frigate *Fregata minor* p. 131
Shape as 1, usually seen soaring over islands.
a, Adult male: black all over, without any white marks
b, Adult female: has equally variable white patch below.
NOTE: Juveniles of both species have white heads, and are virtually indistinguishable.

3. Red-tailed Tropicbird *Phaëthon rubricauda rubricauda* p. 126
White above with few black markings. Bright red bill and tail streamers (absent in young or moulting birds).

4. White-tailed Tropicbird *Phaëthon lepturus lepturus* p. 125
Bill yellow; tail streamers white.

5. Blue-faced (Masked) Booby *Sula dactylatra melanops* p. 130
Heavily built gannet. Predominantly white.
a, Adult: white with trailing edge black for the whole of its length. Large dark patch at base of bill; black tail.
b, Juvenile: dull brown and speckled above, white belly, black tail.

6. Red-footed Booby *Sula sula rubripes* p. 127
a, Adult: as Blue-faced, but black trailing edge does not reach to body; tail white. Conspicuous bright red feet.
b, Juvenile: chocolate brown all over with red feet.

7. Brown Booby *Sula leucogaster* p. 130
Dark brown above, sharply demarcated white area from upper breast to vent; dark tail. See text for distinction from dark-phase Red-footed.

B.S.

BLUE-FACED (MASKED) BOOBY   Fou general
Sula dactylatra melanops   **Pl. 10**
Cos   ?Ass   *Ald*

The same size and general appearance as red-footed, but has the
whole trailing edge of the wing dark, and a dark patch at the
base of the bill. Juvenile has dull brown plumage, with *belly only*
white, tail brown (contrast with brown-phase red-footed, which
has white tail).

The Blue-faced Booby has been seen at Aldabra, but does not
breed there; it breeds on Cosmoledo, and used to on Assumption,
but probably does not do so any longer. Its way of life is like
that of the Red-footed Booby, except that it breeds on the
ground – like a Brown Booby.

Blue-faced Boobies may be seen at sea feeding with groups of
red-footed and very occasionally Brown Boobies (see below).

BROWN BOOBY   Fou capucin   *Sula leucogaster*   **Pl. 10**
Ald   Cos   **Ami**

Dark brown above, white below from chin to vent, broad white
band on under wing. Juvenile has dark brown plumage, paler
where the adult is white, but no white patches.

Seen uncommonly at Aldabra, more often at Cosmoledo, where
it might breed on one of the less-frequented islands. Known to
breed on Desnoeufs in the Amirantes, probably other islands
there as well. Breeds on ground in close colony, single egg,
apparently in June but season may be more extensive.

Distinguished from brown-phase red-footed by dark tail, as
well as white stripe under wing; and from juvenile blue-faced
by greater forward extent of white – and white wing stripe.

ABBOT'S BOOBY   *Sula abbotti*
(ex from **Ass**)

Now restricted to Christmas Island, Abbott's Booby once bred
in mangroves at Assumption. It is a white booby with black

wings, the lower back and rump flecked with black, and the tail black flecked with white. The facial skin is black, but the throat is pale greenish and the feet purple-grey. A record from these waters would create great excitement among ornithologists.

FRIGATEBIRDS

GREAT FRIGATE	Fregate	*Fregata minor*	**Pl. 10**
LESSER FRIGATE	Fregate	*Fregata ariel*	**Pl. 10**

Ald Sey ?**Cos**

Frigatebirds are unmistakable, gaunt and black, most often seen hanging on the wind over islands, especially near their huge breeding colonies at Aldabra. The wings are very long, and the tail deeply forked. The two species here considered are not readily distinguished, but a few pointers may be given. All *juveniles* have white heads, but apart from their size the two species are not separable in the field. All *adults* have black heads: an adult black all over is a male Great Frigate (*Fregata*, unfortunately, *minor*), and an adult black all over save for a small white patch at the base of each wing is a male Lesser Frigate (*F. ariel*). Females have a variable amount of white on the underside, and both species have the throat grey. The female lesser has a small patch of reddish feathers at the base of the neck, but this is almost never visible in flight. Size is the only sure guide to identification, and then only in mixed flocks; in both these species the female is larger than the male.

In central Seychelles the Great Frigate is regularly seen, and the lesser rather more rarely; the lesser becomes more common nearer to the mixed breeding grounds at Aldabra. It is said that the Great Frigate still breeds on Aride, and in 1972 four males were seen displaying there (C. Feare, pers. comm.): both species are said to breed at Cosmoledo, but this also is unconfirmed. Both species are surface feeders, usually far out to sea, diving to skim the sea and pick up squid and flying fish. They are incapable of taking off once they land on the water, partly because of deficient waterproofing of their feathers, and partly because their wings are too long to permit it. This may be the reason for their preference for piracy rather than foraging: they frequently harass boobies and other birds returning from the fishing grounds to make them disgorge their last catch, which the frigate picks out of the air and eats. In this method of feeding, the risk of crashing into the water is reduced; but frigates in pursuit of a booby risk crashing to the ground through an error of aerobatics.

Frigates nest in the miles of mangrove swamps round the lagoon of Aldabra, making untidy platform nests of twigs in crowded colonies along with boobies. The breeding season is from June to December, with a peak between August and October. The males during this time have a grossly distensible red pouch at the base of the bill which they can inflate like a balloon, uttering a quavering wail to attract females. Nest-robbing is rife in the colonies whenever they are disturbed. Each pair lays a single egg, and both parents take part in rearing the young; a curious feature of frigate breeding is that to rear a young bird takes more than a year, because of the protracted period during which the parents feed the chick after it has fledged. This means that frigates can breed only every other year, unless they lose the chick.

The total number of frigates breeding at Aldabra has been estimated by A. W. Diamond as about 30,000 birds, in four major colonies. This figure, coupled with the size of the birds and their habit of soaring over the island at great heights, makes it clear why some of the R.A.F. planners involved in the post-poned scheme for an airbase at Aldabra had reservations about the safety of flying near the atoll.

Non-breeding birds and failed breeders leave Aldabra to range more widely between November and July, when they may be seen commonly in central Seychelles and in the Amirantes.

RARER SEABIRDS – SKUA AND GULLS

GREAT SKUA Poule Mauve *Catharacta skua* **Pl. 11**

From the fact of its having a Créole name, the Great Skua is evidently seen regularly in Seychelles, if only rarely. I saw two on Cousin during the whole of 1970. They are larger than the terns common in Seychelles, and much more heavily built, dark in colour but with pale patches on the wings which are conspicuous in flight. Skuas are very oceanic as a rule, but during the breeding season of other seabirds they will come close to land to take chicks from the breeding colonies, and to harry the adults as they bring food, taking the disgorged food rather in the manner of frigates. Otherwise non-breeding skuas live out of sight of land, taking their food from the surface of the sea in flight. They are solitary, and often follow ships, presumably to benefit both from the discarded refuse and from the disturbed water which might bring prey to the surface. The race of skua seen in the western Indian Ocean breeds far to the south, among the subantarctic islands such as Tristan and Kerguelen. One was seen off Aldabra in November, 1971.

LESSER BLACK-BACKED GULL *Larus fuscus* **Pl. 11**

Gulls are very rare in the Indian Ocean at any distance from land, but the Lesser Black-back has been recorded once in Seychelles (1972), and also at Aldabra (1964). It is unmistakable if only because it looks so large to the eye accustomed to small terns; the wings and mantle are dark grey, the wingtips white; feet and bill are yellow, the bill with a conspicuous red spot. Further records of this species will be very interesting.

BLACK-HEADED GULL *Larus* (probably) *brunnicephalus*
Pl. 11

Black-headed Gulls were unknown in Seychelles until Christmas, 1970, when two records were obtained; two birds were seen on

Frigate on Christmas Day, and six on Mahé a few days later, possibly including those seen on Frigate. More records followed in 1972. These were probably of the Indian species, *L. brunnicephalus*, which breeds from Aden to Ceylon: the difference between this and the northern species, *Larus ridibundus*, is very slight, depending on whether the feet may be described as 'deep red' or 'vermilion' (Alexander) – but on distributional grounds the Indian species is more likely. Further records of these gulls will also be of interest. Out of the breeding season the black on the head is restricted to a spot behind the eye, but the red bill and feet and the white leading edge to the wing are always distinctive.

BRIDLED TERN Francin *Sterna anaethetus antarctica* Pl. 12
Sey Ami Cos

The Bridled Tern is grey-brown on the wings and mantle (its alternative English name is Brown-winged Tern); the head has a black cap and a black 'bridle', a stripe extending from the base of the bill through the eye to join the cap. The white between cap and bridle extends well behind the eye. Bill and feet are black. During the breeding season the adults develop long outer tail feathers. The flight of the Bridled Tern, on its rather broad wings, is stiff-winged with rapid strokes. Its call is a repeated syncopated yap, rather like the bark of a small dog, sometimes referred to as 'laughing'. All these features are to be compared with those given for the Sooty Tern, with which the bridled is readily confused away from the sooty breeding grounds.

The Bridled Tern breeds on rat-free islands, on the ground or on rock ledges under overhangs. The nest is always under cover, either a rock or a tuft of bracken or grass, and the single greenish egg, speckled with brown and purple in very variable patterns, is laid on soil or on a small pile of vegetable debris, never on the bare rock. (Compare with the Fairy Tern, whose eggs may be very similar.) Breeding is synchronous within a colony, but the season seems to be locally determined, or perhaps non-annual. On Cousin in 1970 the Bridled Terns bred in May to August;

Vesey-Fitzgerald found eggs in January on Recif, and in October on Cosmoledo in 1939 and 1940. The chick is chocolate-brown, and highly nidifugous from the first day of life. The parents – and the patient bird-watcher – can locate it by its hoarse piping call. The juvenile plumage is a muted and fuzzy version of the adult: the head is streaky iron-grey, and the back is finely barred brown and white. The wings in the first plumage are pearl-grey with darker primaries.

Bridled Terns are surface-feeders seldom far from land, and unlike the Sooty Tern they are non-migratory, so that there are always some to be seen around the islands. They roost at night in dense flocks either on bare rock slopes or high in trees.

SOOTY TERN   Goelette   *Sterna fuscata nubilosa*   Pl. 12
Sey   Ami   Cos   Ast

The wings and mantle of the Sooty Tern are black, and although the cap and bridle are much the same as in the Bridled Tern, the white extends less far behind the eye. The flight of the sooty is slower, with more flexible wing strokes, its wings appearing longer and narrower than those of the Bridled Tern – the sooty is in fact much the larger bird. The tail streamers grown during breeding are longer in the sooty. The voice is a nasal three-syllabled call 'waanyiwaa', interpreted by some people as 'wideawake'.

Out of the breeding season the sooty may be seen almost any-where in the Indian Ocean as it roams in flocks; but during the season (about May to October) the birds congregate round the breeding islands. The biggest colony is at Desnoeufs in the Amirantes, where there are still over a million pairs; the next is at Bird Island, close to the central granitic group, where a colony of 2,500 pairs has been encouraged by the owners until now it numbers at least half a million. Other colonies, smaller but still flourishing, are on Aride (and two which may now be defunct on Recif and Mamelles, both heavily poached), and on African Banks in the Amirantes. There are small colonies also at Astove,

Cosmoledo, and Farquhar, and flocks of sooties have been seen round Aldabra, but there is no sign that they breed there. The sooty is a surface feeder, usually well out to sea, taking small fish.

The nesting season of sooties seems to be determined by the onset of the south-east monsoon, in late April or early May, when the flocks begin to congregate round the islands for breeding. The territories are determined when the eggs are laid in June, when each bird defends the area round it for as far as it can reach while sitting. This produces a strikingly even array of eggs on the ground. The chicks hatch in August, and are fed by the parents for about eight weeks. The din in the colony is astonishing, a constant high-pitched hiss from the combined effect of a million shrill calls. Amidst all this noise, the parents have been shown to identify their own chicks by differences in voice from others nearby. In September the young birds are flying, and the crowd in the air becomes even more dense, and then by the end of October the colonies are deserted while the birds range over the ocean until the next season.

The eggs of the Sooty Tern are large and palatable, and they have been cropped for many years, with some damage to the famous colony on Desneoufs; but now there are strict rules governing the collecting season and the numbers collected from various parts of the colony, and there is every hope that the colony will not decline further. The high density of nesting, which has made the Sooty Tern such an easy bird for man to parasitise, is very effective in protecting it from its natural enemies such as herons and frigatebirds, which dare not enter the colony itself to take chicks and eggs, but can only make occasional forays at the edges. On Ascension Island, in the Atlantic, however, one or two rogue frigates have been known to cause great carnage in parts of the Sooty Tern colony, taking dozens of chicks a day. This has never been observed in the Indian Ocean colonies.

ROSEATE TERN Diamant (one of several) *Sterna*
dougallii arideensis   **Pl. 12**
Sey Ami

The Roseate Tern is another grey-winged, black-capped small
tern, recognisable by its bill, bright red at the base with a black
tip of variable length, and its feet, varying from red to orange
depending on the breeding condition of the bird. Birds in
breeding condition have the underparts suffused with deep pink,
which makes them unmistakable. The call of the Roseate Tern
is a short staccato yelp, like a small dog, but given singly, not in
series like the call of the Bridled Tern. Another recognition
feature usually given for the species is its deeply forked tail, but
this is not always visible in flight, if the tail is folded.

The Roseate Tern breeds on Aride (from which the local subspecies has its name), Mamelles, and Recif, as well as on some
of the numerous small islets off the coast of Mahé and Praslin.
One of these, Ile aux Vaches Marines, off Grand'Anse Mahé, is
a reserve. There is no breeding season as such, eggs being found
all the year round, but there is a peak in breeding during the
south-east monsoon. The roseate is a surface feeder, close inshore
as a rule.

The eggs are laid on soil, not on bare rock, sometimes with
traces of nest material; they have been found on bare sand in
the Amirantes, where there is a breeding colony on African
Banks* – and probably on other small islands which have never
been searched. The clutch is almost always one, as for the other
small terns in the area, but two have been reported on occasion.
The chicks are dark-coloured, nidifugous.

The Roseate Tern is a world-wide species, breeding from
Maine to Scotland across the Atlantic, and in the Pacific and
Indian Oceans as well. In the Indian Ocean there are no fewer
than four recognised subspecies, of which this is the most limited
in range. Over the rest of the world there is only one other
subspecies.

*In the African Banks colony, the Roseate Tern has no black tip at all to its bill.

Note. Diamant is a generic Créole name for all small terns of this type.

BLACK-NAPED TERN   Diamant   *Sterna sumatrana mathewsi*   **Pl. 12**
Ald   Ast   Ami

Smaller and paler in colour than the Roseate Tern, the Black-naped Tern has a very long forked tail, and a black band round the back of the head. The bill and feet are black, but the bill has a lighter tip which is sometimes visible in the field.

The Black-naped Tern breeds on Astove, and African Banks in the Amirantes, and at Aldabra, but not in central Seychelles. The breeding season given by Alexander is exactly opposite to that observed at Aldabra, where egg-laying was mainly in January and February, but extended from November to March. (Alexander gives May to December as the egg-dates.) The species is a surface-feeder, in the lagoon or over the reef-front, not in deep water; it takes small fish.

The nest in the Amirantes, and on Providence and Farquhar, is usually in sand or shingle, a simple scrape, but on Aldabra it is on bare rocky islets, perhaps because the rest of the atoll is overrun with rats. A small bundle of vegetation bears one or quite often two eggs (ten out of twenty-eight nests had two eggs at Aldabra in 1967, according to A. W. Diamond). The nests were usually single, or sometimes in groups of two or three together.

Recent observations suggest that Black-naped Terns might soon begin breeding on Bird Island, which is now a strict sanctuary for sea birds. Ninety were seen there together in October, 1970. The species is not rare, breeding on coral islands all over the Indian and Pacific Oceans.

LITTLE TERN   Diamant   *Sterna albifrons*   **Pl. 12**
(breeding place in Indian Ocean not known)   *Sey   Ald*   (Ami)

The Little Tern is very small indeed, with a black cap, and a dark leading edge to an otherwise pale grey wing. The rump and tail are grey, the bill yellow with a black tip, the feet yellow. So far it has not been found breeding in the area covered by this account, but it is commonly seen in central Seychelles and at Aldabra, and probably regular also in the Amirantes.

Little Terns feed along the edge of the sea, often where waves are breaking on a beach, with a very fluttering and agile flight; they roost in flocks on sand banks at low tide.

DAMARA TERN Lascar *Sterna balaenarum*
Ami Sey

Although the Damara Tern is classically described as a bird of the coasts of west Africa, there is a population of a small tern which fits the description of the Damara in the Amirantes, notably on African Island, and also on Bird Island in the outer Seychelles. These birds differ from Little Terns in having the bill black for the whole of its length, the forehead black, and the outermost primaries very dark grey. In addition the middle tail feathers are pearly grey and the outer feathers white. Peterson, Shackleton, and other authorities who are familiar with the species are in no doubt of the identification. The first record in Seychelles was in April, 1970, at Cousin Island, where the call was heard – a sharp 'whip whip' as the bird fed among the surf on the beach. These small terns show great agility of flight, even more than the Little Tern.

Damara Tern *Sterna balaenarum*

Their positive identification must await the collection of specimens, which has so far not been possible. The largest group seen on African Island numbered eighty-six in October, 1971, and on Bird Island ninety or more in May, 1970.

It might be significant that among all the small terns that frequent the waters round the Amirantes, this species has a Créole name that is not 'Diamant', the common name for all small terns.

As yet no positive record of breeding exists, but further investigation of the Amirantes may yet yield proof that this is a new subspecies of the Damara Tern.

FAIRY TERN Goeland blanc *Gygis alba monte*   **Pl. 12**
Sey Ami Ald

Pure white all over, with darker shafts to the primaries in fresh dress, and a bright blue base to the black upturned bill, the Fairy (or White) Tern is quite unmistakable. Round the smaller islands in Seychelles, and in the Amirantes, it is very common; at Aldabra, where the breeding population is estimated at about 300 pairs, it is less conspicuous. It also breeds in small numbers at Assumption. Its call is a curious twanging quack, repeated loudly and endlessly in the dense breeding colonies; it also utters a shrill whistle when alarmed.

The Fairy Tern is rarely seen out of sight of land; at Ascension Island, according to Dorward (1963), it feeds away from the shore, and Diamond makes a point of saying that it feeds outside the reef at Aldabra; but in Seychelles it feeds close inshore much of the time, though it is not uncommon in the channel between Mahé and Praslin. I have seen birds flying into the lamplight in Seychelles in the middle of moonless nights carrying fish, so apparently they can feed at night, perhaps locating their prey by its phosphorescent track in the water. There being no breeding season, Fairy Terns are common during the whole year round the islands where they breed.

The Fairy Tern nests on trees or rocks without the vestige of a

nest, laying its rather spherical egg directly on to a perch where
its balance looks most precarious. The egg varies in colour from
green to blue, and the size and density of brown and purple
spots on it, together with scrawling and large even blotches, are
all variable to a degree, so that no one egg looks like another.
The sitting bird is very tame, probably because leaving the egg
is a risky business, not only because of the danger of dislodging it,
but because the Toq Toq (page 117) is such an avid predator.
The chick when it hatches has enormous feet, which enable it to
hang on to perches which even the tree-nesting Noddy Terns
cannot use. Both parents feed the young with fish carried in the
bill, not regurgitated, the size of the fish being accurately graded
to match the size of the chick. Newly fledged young birds lack
the blue base to the bill, and for the first few weeks they have
distinct brown markings on the back, but these soon wear off.

The numbers of the Fairy Tern in central Seychelles, where it
was once the most common sea bird, have been much reduced
since 1950 by the African Barn Owl, introduced in an abortive
attempt to control rats. Now Fairy Terns are a rare sight off
Mahé or Praslin, though on the other islands they survive in
numbers. The breeding group on Cousin probably numbers
10,000 pairs.

LESSER (BLACK) NODDY Cordonnier *Anous*
tenuirostris tenuirostris   **Pl. 11**

COMMON (BROWN) NODDY Maqua *Anous*
stolidus pileatus   **Pl. 11**
Former **Sey** only; latter **Sey** **Ald** **Ami**

In central Seychelles these two species are closely similar in their
way of life as well as in their appearance, so it seems best to take
them together here; but it should be noted that only the Common
(Brown) Noddy occurs elsewhere in the area.

Both are dark grey terns with white head patches: the Lesser
Noddy is smaller and more slightly built, with a relatively longer
and much more slender bill. In strong sunlight it looks charcoal

grey; the patch on the head extends nearly to the nape. Its flight is more fluttery and hesitant, with quick wing-beats. The Common Noddy is nearly twice the size of the Lesser, heavily built, with a relatively short stout bill. In strong light the back and scapulars look *brown*, in contrast to the black primaries, and although the extent of the head-patch is variable, it is usually confined to the front part of the crown, extending farther only in very young birds. The fore-edge, above the eye, is sharply delineated, giving the species a 'stern look'. The flight of the Common Noddy is strong and direct, and its movements in a mixed flock appear smoother and more deliberate than those of the Lessers hovering around it. The tail of the Common Noddy is relatively much longer than that of the Lesser. The calls are similar, but that of the Common Noddy is deeper, like the cry of a raven, while the lesser gives a high-pitched rattle.

The Lesser Noddy nests in trees, in dense colonies of small compact nests, made of dead leaves of *Pisonia* (see below) and algae collected wet from the sea. The mucus running down from the algae cements the nest together like a plug of tobacco. One small white egg is laid, soon to become so dirty as almost to hide the sparse purple and brown speckling on it.

The Common Noddy, on the other hand, nests most often in rocks or in coconut palms, in small groups in central Seychelles (but in dense crowded colonies on the ground in other places). Its nest is most often made of dry materials, including bracken stems and grass, and the large egg remains clean and white, with a similar pattern to that of the Lesser. The chick of the Common Noddy is covered in pearl-grey down, whereas that of the Lesser (or Black) Noddy is black. Whereas the Lesser Noddy has no marked breeding season, but a peak in May and again in December, the Common Noddy breeds almost exclusively during the calms following the north-west monsoon, beginning in May, and carrying on through the start of the south-east monsoon in August. At Aldabra the Common Noddy breeds from December to March on rocky islets in the lagoon.

In both species the parents feed the chick on regurgitated

small fish, caught close to the surface in fairly deep water some way from land. The chicks of both species fledge quite rapidly, in about seven weeks, and in both species there is quite a protracted 'apprenticeship period' during which the fledged chick returns to the nest or nearby to roost although it is often away during the day.

Chicks which fall from the nests may occasionally be fed by the parents – sometimes more than one pair – but most often they fall prey to crabs very quickly. I have seen a Common Noddy carrying a fallen new-hatched chick back up to the nest in the rocks above, but the Lesser is said never to do this.

Apart from predation by lizards and birds, noddies on small islands in Seychelles are prone to death by entanglement with the fruits of the tree *Pisonia grandis*, which are very sticky as an aid to dispersal. Large numbers of noddies seeking nesting material, mostly lessers, are to be found dying on the ground completely flightless after being trapped by the fruits. *Pisonia* (*bois mapou*) fruits twice in a year, for only a short period, but during this time some hundreds of noddies were killed from the 10,000-strong colony on Cousin Island.

Another, diminishing, source of loss to noddies is the collection of their eggs for human consumption, especially in the Amirantes, where they breed on the same islands as the huge numbers of Sooty Terns.

The three Lesser Noddy colonies in Seychelles, on Cousin, Cousine, and the huge one on Aride, are the only breeding places of this subspecies, though other subspecies are common elsewhere in the Indian Ocean.

CRESTED TERN Goeland sardine *Thalasseus bergii* **Pl. 12**
Ald Ami ?**Ast** *Sey*

The Crested Tern is a fairly large black-capped grey-backed tern with a white forehead; the bill is yellow and the legs black; the tail is deeply forked. The black feathers of the crown are elongated into a crest, which is visible when the bird is settled.

Plate 11   SKUA, GULLS, GULL-BILLED TERN
AND NODDIES

1. Great Skua   *Catharacta skua*   p. 133
Large, heavily-built, gull-shaped bird. Dark with light
patches at base of primaries.

2. Lesser Black-backed Gull   *Larus fuscus*   p. 133
White with dark grey wings having white outline on upper
surface, white 'mirrors' on black tips.

3. Black-headed Gull   *Larus brunnicephalus*   p. 133
Small gull, wings light grey with white leading edge, white
'mirrors' as **2.** Out of breeding season carries small dark
patch behind eye; in breeding, whole head is dark brown.

4. Gull-billed Tern   *Geochelidon nilotica*   p. 146
Very pale grey on back; black bill and large eye. Readily
confused with Fairy Tern (Plate 12), but feeds quite differ-
ently, and close view reveals darker colour.

5. Lesser (Black) Noddy   *Anous tenuirostris tenuirostris*   p. 141
Small, all-black tern with light patch on forehead; long
slender bill.
a, In flight: rather fluttery and hesitant; no noticeable wing
pattern.
b, On ground: showing size comparison with Common
Noddy.

6. Common (Brown) Noddy   *Anous stolidus pileatus*   p. 141
Larger and longer-tailed than Lesser Noddy.
a, In flight: direct and confident: upper wing noticeably
brown on coverts, black at tip. Patch on forehead sharply
delineated, bill sturdy.
b, On ground: for relative size to Lesser Noddy.

1. **Lesser Crested Tern** *Thalasseus bengalensis* p. 146
Individual shown is non-breeding bird: in breeding dress
the cap is black right to the bill.

2. **Crested Tern** *Thalasseus bergii* p. 143
Very similar to 1, but larger and darker-coloured, especially
on wing-tips.

3. **Black-naped Tern** *Sterna sumatrana mathewsi* p. 138
Small, pale-coloured tern, with very long, forked tail in
flight. Black band round back of head. Bill and feet black.

4. **Caspian Tern** *Hydroprogne caspia* p. 147
Huge, grey-backed, black-capped tern, with bright red bill,
black feet. Under wing-tips dark, distinguishing it from
Lesser Crested at distance in flight.

5. **Fairy Tern** *Gygis alba monte* p. 140
Pure white, small tern, with slightly upcurved black bill,
blue at base in adults: feet black. Enormous black eye.

6. **Bridled Tern** *Sterna anaethetus antarctica* p. 134
Brownish-grey (not black) on wings and mantle, black cap
and line through eye. Bill and feet black.

7. **Sooty Tern** *Sterna fuscata nubilosa* p. 135
Jet black on wings and mantle.

8. **Roseate Tern** *Sterna dougallii arideensis* p. 137
Black cap complete; wings and mantle darker grey than
Black-naped. Bill red. with black tip in Seychelles but not
in Amirantes. Feet red or orange.

9. **Little Tern** *Sterna albifrons* p. 138
Very small, black cap, dark leading edge to pale grey wing.
Bill yellow with black tip; feet yellow. Forehead white in
breeding dress.

B.S. K

The Crested Tern is common at Aldabra, where it breeds in July, but apparently also sometimes in January. It breeds also May to September on African Banks in the Amirantes, and possibly also on Astove, but although it is not uncommon in central Seychelles it does not breed there. It feeds in shallow water, over flats covered in 'turtle grass', taking small fish.

The nest is a simple scrape, containing one egg, usually in coarse sand at the top of a beach. The parents are brave in defence of the nest, attacking repeatedly when disturbed.

There were at least fifty-four pairs of Crested Terns breeding at Aldabra in 1969. The species is not rare; its range covers the whole of the Indian and Pacific Oceans.

LESSER CRESTED TERN   *Thalasseus bengalensis*   Pl. 12

(Breeding place among the islands not known)   *Ald*

The Lesser Crested Tern is distinguished from the crested by its *orange* not yellow bill, black forehead in breeding dress (May to August), and smaller size, as well as its somewhat paler colour. Although it is seen regularly round Aldabra it does not seem to breed there; the nearest breeding grounds given by Alexander are in east Africa, where the species breeds in June and July. There has been no record of the species either from Seychelles or the Amirantes.

The Lesser Crested Tern feeds in the lagoon at Aldabra, and also outside the reef in deep water.

GULL-BILLED TERN   *Gelochelidon nilotica*   Pl. 11
Sey

The Gull-billed Tern is readily confused in flight with the Fairy Tern, since it appears white all over, with a conspicuous black bill. At closer range, however, the black streaks on top of the head can be seen, and the pale grey of the wings and tail. The most striking feature which distinguishes it from the fairy, though, is its method of feeding, diving headlong towards very shallow water, such as the edges of the reclaim in Victoria

Harbour, to pick up crabs and other small prey from the surface. The bill, as its name suggests, is shorter and stouter than that of most terns. This species was first recorded for Seychelles by M. Harris in December, 1971, but since then several have been seen, and it may be that the mud and stony flats of the reclaim have provided a feeding ground which was hitherto lacking in the area. Further records would be of great interest, at sea as well as by land.

CASPIAN TERN *Hydroprogne caspia* Pl. 12
Ald   ??**Ast**

The Caspian Tern is unmistakable for its size alone – it is the largest tern to be seen in these waters. It is grey-backed and black-capped, with a huge red bill. There are usually one or two to be seen round the lagoon at Aldabra, especially during the breeding season, April to August. It has also been seen at Astove, where it might breed, and at Cosmoledo, where apparently it does not. Its call is a harsh scream, especially when disturbed, for example from a nest. It has never been recorded in Seychelles. The Caspian Tern feeds in shallow water, taking fish of quite a fair size. In an unusual encounter, one was robbed by a Dimorphic Egret, which darted at it as the tern seized a fish from close by, causing the tern to drop the fish, which the heron ate. The water in that place was only about two inches deep.

The nest is a scrape at the top of a beach, the clutch one egg. The parents, like Crested Terns, are defiant in defence of the nest; on account of their large size, they are rather more daunting to the finder of the nest.

Migrant Shorebirds

The following waders have been recorded from the islands covered by this book, mostly in the northern winter (October to March). Some, such as the turnstone and the whimbrel, regularly summer south, and may be present in the islands all the year round. Except where another Créole name is given, these birds are all known to the Seychellois as 'Zallouettes'. Regular migrants are marked with an asterisk.

*Siberian Ringed Plover	Ald Sey	*Charadrius hiaticula tundrae*
Little Ringed Plover	Sey	*Ch. dubius*
Lesser Sand Plover	Ast Sey	*Ch. mongolus atrifrons*
*Great Sand Plover	Ald Sey	*Ch. leschenaultii*
Caspian Plover	Sey	*Ch. asiaticus*
Asiatic Golden Plover	Sey	*Ch. dominica fulva*
*Grey Plover	Ald Sey	*Pluvialis squatarola*
*Turnstone (*Baise Roche*)	Ald Sey	*Arenaria interpres*
Little Stint	Ald Sey	*Calidris minuta*
*Curlew Sandpiper	Ald Sey Ami	*C. ferruginea*
Great Knot	Sey	*C. tenuirostris*
*Sanderling	Ald Sey	*C. alba*
Greenshank	Ald Sey	*Tringa nebularia*
Redshank	Sey	*T. totanus*
Spotted Redshank	Sey (Coetivy)	*T. erythropus*
*Wood Sandpiper	Ald Sey	*T. glareola*
Marsh Sandpiper	Sey	*T. stagnatilis*
*Common Sandpiper	Ald Sey	*T. hypoleucos*
*Terek Sandpiper	Ald Sey	*Xenus cinereus*
*Bar-tailed Godwit	Ald Sey	*Limosa lapponica lapponica*
?*Common Curlew (*Courli*)	Ald	*Numenius arquata (orientalis)*
Slender-billed Curlew (*Courli*)	Ald	*N. tenuirostris*
*Whimbrel (*Corbijeau*)	Ald Sey	*N. phaeopus phaeopus*
Snipe	Sey	*Gallinago media*
Grey (U.S.=Red) Phalarope	Sey	*Phalaropus fulicarius*
*Crab Plover (*Cavalier*)	Ald Sey	*Dromas ardeola*
Eastern Collared Pratincole	Sey	*Glareola maldivarum*

I am much indebted to Chris Feare and Tony Beamish for passing on some of these records. There are bound to be more as the number of competent observers grows – use the margins to fill them in, and take steps to publish the observation.

Migrants and Vagrants other than Shorebirds

The following species have been recorded from Aldabra (A), the Amirantes (Ami), or Seychelles (S). Because there have been few observers in the past, these records are surely incomplete, and it is not possible in most cases to say whether the birds are regular migrants or merely vagrants. Some species have been seen only once; where for various reasons (e.g. the Broad-billed Roller has a Créole name) the species might be regular, this too is shown. All unexpected birds should be recorded very carefully, with provisional identification and accurate description, and preferably a copy of the record should be lodged either with the Smithsonian Institution or at the British Museum (Natural History) at Tring, with a copy left in Seychelles.

Night Heron *Nycticorax nycticorax*

English name	Scientific name	Status where known	Place
Night Heron	*Nycticorax nycticorax*	Once	A
African Sacred Ibis	*Threskiornis ae. aethiopica*	Once	A
White-faced Tree Duck	*Dendrocygna viduata*	Once	A
Black Kite	*Milvus migrans*	?Reg	A
Marsh Harrier	*Circus ae. aeruginosus*	Once	S
Falcons	*Falco* spp	Reg	A/S

eleanorae has been identified in Seychelles once (November, 1971) and is likely at Aldabra; *concolor* is regular in Seychelles and also likely at Aldabra

Striped Crake	*Porzana marginalis*	Once	A
Grey Cuckoo	*Cuculus canorus*	?Reg	A/S
Lesser Cuckoo	*C. poliocephalus*	?Reg	S
Eurasian Swift	*Apus apus*	Reg	A/?S/Ami
European Roller	*Coracias garrulus*	Once	A
		Reg	S
Broad-billed Roller	*Eurystomus glaucurus*	Reg	A/Ami
('*Katiti madagascar*')		?Once	Sey
Blue-cheeked Bee-eater	*Merops superciliosus*	Once	A
Sand Martin	*Riparia riparia*	More than once	A
Mascarene Martin	*Phedina borbonica*	Once	A
European Swallow	*Hirundo rustica*	?Reg	A
		Once	S
Yellow-throated Longclaw	*Macronyx croceus*	Once	Ami
Pipits	*Anthus* spp	Once	A
Tree Pipit	*A. trivialis*	Identified once in Sey	
Yellow Wagtail	*Motacilla flava*	More than once	A
Lesser Grey Shrike	*Lanius minor*	Once	A
Golden Oriole	*Oriolus oriolus*	Once	A
European Willow Warbler	*Phylloscopus trochilus*	Twice	Ami
Spotted Flycatcher	*Muscicapa striata*	?Reg	A
Wheatear	*Oenanthe oenanthe*	?Reg	A
		Once	S
Rock Thrush	*Monticola saxatilis*	Once	S

In addition to these records, an African Scops Owl, probably *Otus scops senegalensis*, was captured alive on board a ship 150 miles north of Seychelles in November, 1967. A vagrant roller of unknown species was shot in Seychelles in November, 1970, but the carcass was lost; from the description from the man who shot it, it was almost certainly a Broad-billed Roller, which would have been the first record in Seychelles.

Unidentified birds of prey are regularly reported in Seychelles during the northern winter months, including one record which suggested a species of *Buteo*, possibly *B. buteo* – but the description was just not detailed enough. Photograph and describe all unknown birds – your record is almost certain to be new to science.

Purple Heron *Ardea purpurea*
Seen once on Praslin, December, 1970

APPENDIX III

Select Bibliography
in chronological order

(a) *Local ornithological*

NEWTON, E. 1867. Descriptions of some new birds from the Seychelles Islands. *Proc. Zool. Soc. Lond.* 1867: 344–7.

NEWTON, E. 1867a. On the land birds of the Seychelles Archipelago. *Ibis* (2) *3*: 335–60.

OUSTALET, M. E. 1878. Etude sur la faune ornithologique des îles Seychelles. *Bull. Soc. philomath. Paris* (7) *2*: 161–206.

Abbott's visit

ABBOTT, W. L. 1893. Notes on the natural history of Aldabra, Assumption, and Glorioso Islands. *Proc. U.S. nat. Mus. 16*: 759–64.

BENDIRE, C. 1894. Descriptions of nests and eggs of some new birds collected on the island of Aldabra . . . *Proc. U.S. nat. Mus. 17*: 39–41.

RIDGWAY, R. 1895. On birds collected by Dr W. L. Abbott . . . *Ibid 18*: 509–46.

Nicoll's visit

NICOLL, M. J. 1906. On the birds collected and observed during the voyage of the 'Valhalla' . . . *Ibis*: (8) *6*: 666–712.

NICOLL, M. J. 1908. *Three Voyages of a Naturalist*. London: Witherby.

Later workers

VESEY-FITZGERALD, L. D. E. F. 1940. The birds of the Seychelles. I: The endemic birds. *Ibis* (14) *4*: 480–9.

VESEY-FITZGERALD, L. D. E. F. 1941. Further contributions to the ornithology of the Seychelles Islands. *Ibis* (14) *5*: 518–21.

WHITE, C. M. N. 1951. Systematic notes on African birds. *Ibis 93*: 460–5.

CROOK, J. H. 1961. The Fodies (Ploceinae) of the Seychelles. *Ibis 103a*: 517–48.

LOUSTAU-LALANNE, P. L. 1962. Land birds of the granitic islands of the Seychelles. *Occ. Publs. Seychelles Soc.* 1. Pp. 32.

LOUSTAU-LALANNE, P. L. 1963. Sea and shore birds of the Seychelles. *Occ. Publs. Seychelles Soc.* 2. Pp. 26.

WATSON, G. E. *et al.* 1963. *Preliminary Field Guide to the Birds of the Indian Ocean.* Washington: Smithsonian Institution. Pp. 214.

Bristol Seychelles Expedition

GAYMER, R. 1965. The islands' endangered species. *Animals 6*: 544–7.

PENNY, M. J. 1965. Studying the rare birds of Cousin. 58–60; The Black Parrots of Praslin. 184–7; The Seychelles Black Paradise Flycatcher. 304–6; The Birds of Aldabra. 407–9. *Animals 7.*

DAWSON, P. G. 1965. Frigate, home of the Magpie Robin. *Animals 7*: 520–2.

BLACKMAN, R. A. A. 1965. Biological control (the Barn Owl). *Animals 8*: 72–4.

PENNY, M. J. 1967. A new sanctuary in Seychelles. 214–16; (1968) Endemic birds of the Seychelles. 267–75. *Oryx 9.*

GAYMER, R., BLACKMAN, R. A. A. *et al.* 1966. The endemic birds of Seychelles. *Ibis 111*: 157–76.

Royal Society Expedition to Aldabra

BENSON, C. W., and PENNY, M. J. 1967. A new species of warbler from the Aldabra Atoll. *Bull. B.O.C. 88*: 102–8.

STODDART, D. R. (ed.) 1970. Coral islands of the Western Indian Ocean. *Atoll. Res. Bull. 136*: 1–224.

BENSON, C. W. and PENNY, M. J. 1971. The land birds of Aldabra. *Phil. Trans. Roy. Soc. Lond.* B. *260*: 417–527.

PENNY, M. J. and DIAMOND, A. W. 1971. The White-throated Rail at Aldabra. *Ibid*: 529–48.

PENNY, M. J. 1971. Migrant waders at Aldabra . . . *Ibid*: 549–59.

DIAMOND, A. W. 1971. The ecology of the sea birds at Aldabra. *Ibid*: 561–71.

(b) *General*

ALEXANDER, W. B. 1928. *Birds of the Ocean.* London: Putnam.

BAKER, B. H. and MILLER, J. A. 1963. Geology and Geochronology of the Seychelles Islands . . . *Nature 199*: 346–8.

BEAMISH, H. H. 1970. *Aldabra Alone.* London: George Allen and Unwin.

CARLQUIST, S. 1965. *Island Life.* New York, N.Y.: Doubleday.

MACARTHUR, R. O. and WILSON, E. O. 1967. *The theory of island biogeography*. Princeton: University of Princeton Press.

OMMANEY, F. D. 1952. *The Shoals of Capricorn*. London: Longmans Green.

SAUER, J. D. 1967. *Plants and Man on the Seychelles Coast*. London: University of Wisconsin Press.

THOMAS, A. 1968. *Forgotten Eden*. London: Longmans.

TRAVIS, W. 1959. *Beyond the Reefs*. London: George Allen and Unwin.

Index

Créole names are marked with an asterisk. Figures in **bold** type refer to pages opposite plates on which the birds are illustrated.

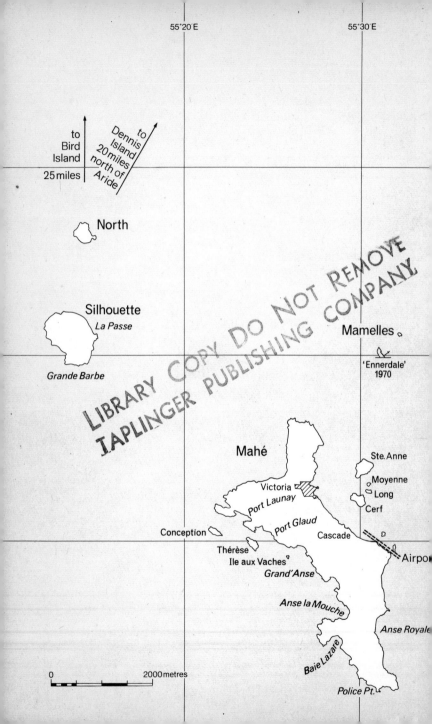

55°20'E   55°30'E

to
Bird
Island

to
Dennis
Island
20 miles
north of
Aride

25 miles

North

Silhouette

La Passe

Grande Barbe

Mamelles

'Ennerdale'
1970

Mahé

Ste. Anne

Moyenne

Victoria

Long

Port Launay

Cerf

Port Glaud

Conception

Cascade

Thérèse
Ile aux Vaches

Airpo

Grand'Anse

Anse la Mouche

Anse Royale

Baie Lazare

0   2000 metres

Police Pt.